THE STRUGGLES, CHALLENGES, AND TRIUMPHS OF THE AFRICAN IMMIGRANTS IN AMERICA

THE STRUGGLES, CHALLENGES, AND TRIUMPHS OF THE AFRICAN IMMIGRANTS IN AMERICA

Darlington Iheonunekwu Iheanacho Ndubuike

Symposium Series
Volume 67

The Edwin Mellen Press
Lewiston•Queenston•Lampeter

Library of Congress Cataloging-in-Publication Data

Ndubuike, Darlington Iheonunekwu Iheanacho.
  The struggles, challenges, and triumphs of the African immigrants in America /
Darlington Iheonunekwu Iheanacho Ndubuike.
      p. cm. -- (Symposium series ; v. 67)
  Includes bibliographical references and index.
  ISBN 0-7734-7076-X
    1. Africans--United States--Social life and customs. 2. Africans--United States--Social
conditions. 3. Africans--Ethnic identity--United States. 4. Immigrants--United
States--Social life and customs. 5. Immigrants--United States--Social conditions. 6.
Blacks--United States--Social life and customs. 7. Blacks--United States--Social
conditions. 8. United States--Emigration and immigration. 9. Africa--Emigration and
immigration. I. Title. II. Symposium series (Edwin Mellen Press) ; v. 67.

E184.A24 N48 2002
305.896'073--dc21

                                                                          2002071820

This is volume 67 in the continuing series
Symposium Series
Volume 67 ISBN 0-7734-7076-X
SS Series ISBN 0-88946-989-X

A CIP catalog record for this book is available from the British Library.

         The Edwin Mellen Press   The Edwin Mellen Press
                Box 450   Box 67
           Lewiston, New York   Queenston, Ontario
            USA 14092-0450   CANADA L0S 1L0

                        The Edwin Mellen Press, Ltd.
                        Lampeter, Ceredigion, Wales
                        UNITED KINGDOM SA48 8LT

                     Printed in the United States of America

To my wife, Patience Ody and my children, Valentine Kelechi, Candice Chika, Leslie Chidinma, and Valerie Onyinyechi

CONTENTS

Foreword

In recent years, the United States and Particularly Texas has witnessed a phenomenal expansion and/or growth in the cultural diversity of its population. As can be expected, this abundance of cultures and ethnicities has presented tremendous challenges and opportunities to professionals and scholars. Colleges and Universities are increasingly striving to produce graduates equipped with international understanding, cultural sensitivity, knowledge, and skills that will enable them to participate in our global society. **The Struggles, Challenges, and Triumphs of the African Immigrants in America** provides a cost-effective tool to assist academic institutions in their efforts to achieve these goals.

In the past, many school systems and institutions of higher learning have neglected, at great cost, the importance of cultural diversity and African Studies in the ever-fast increasing interdependent world. The relative neglect of the study of Africa in American secondary and higher education is a grievous oversight that must be remedied. It not only undermines our effort to understand African contributions to world civilization but also our ability to appreciate distinctively African contributions to early American culture and African American contributions to present-day America.

Dr. Ndubuike's book recognizes the importance of providing the younger generation with knowledge about other parts of our interdependent world, including Africa. Therefore, in providing teachers with an in-depth knowledge of Africa, or enhancing it where it already exists, Dr. Ndubuike aims not only at introducing Africa in the school curriculum, but also helping to improve cultural sensitivities to the history, culture, and traditions of the African people. The book not only presents a historical overview of the immigration of this African immigrant group, but it also provided an in-depth analysis of the totality of their way of life, thus creating insight into the understanding of the cultures of others.

The book examines deeply the culture of the African immigrants in America, their rituals of identity, their struggles, challenges, and triumphs, providing the readers with information needed to understand the culture of this immigrant group and availing them with the opportunity to make multi-cultural and cross-cultural comparisons.

Fredoline O. Anunobi
Associate Professor and Head
Division of Social Work, Behavioral & Political Sciences
Prairie View A & M University

Preface

In recent years, Africans have come to America in large numbers and have settled in different cities and states across the United States. In education and business and through activities, festivals, and cultural exhibitions, they have continued to make their mark on their new land.

Takaki (1993) points to the need for every student in America to know more about the origins and history of the cultures that they will encounter during their lives. Looking at this immigrant group from a multicultural perspective will afford us all the opportunity to comparatively analyze their experiences and be able to develop an understanding of their differences and similarities. Embracing the nation's cultural diversity is a necessity because America derives its strength from it (Takaki, 1993).

There is, therefore, a need for greater understanding of the cultures and experiences of this African immigrant group residing in the United States. The chapters following will examine the culture of the African immigrant groups in America, their family orientation, rituals and symbols of identity, and their responses to the pushes and pulls of this dominant, foreign culture. The discussion will be based on both empirical findings and observational writings since much less literature is available on the recent African immigrants in America.

African art is also examined in this volume because understanding the art of different cultures makes diversity possible without a shock. Art communicates across language and cultural barriers, and reaches that which is fundamental in human nature. Its images and sound, says Grigsby (1989), speak to, move, and touch people of all backgrounds and cultures.

The culture of the Africans in America is worth studying, and there has not been a better time to do so than now when multicultural education has captured the interest of America and the rest of the world. What will be documented here is not the history of the African peoples. The main focus of the researcher is to examine the cultural orientation of the African immigrants in transition and document their rituals and symbols of identity.

Although Africans can be found all over the United States, one of the areas where their influence is strongly felt is in Houston, which has experienced a great influx of Africans over the years. This may be due primarily to the presence of one of America's biggest Black Institutions, Texas Southern University. One African immigrant group nostalgically referred to it as "the University of Nigeria in Houston."

The Houston area has perhaps one of the largest and most diverse populations in the Unites States of immigrants born in African. It is estimated that over 30, 000 Africans reside in Houston. This number includes Africans from Nigeria, Ghana, Ethiopia, Gambia, Somalia, Liberia, Sierra Leone, Togo, Senegal, Eritrea, Cameron, Tanzania, Ivory Coast, Kenya, Uganda, and many other African countries, and all these groups have their individual organizations.

The Washington, D. C. region also has a large population of African immigrants with over 60, 000 people (Selassie, 1996). Substantial number of African immigrants could also be found in Atlanta, Dallas, Baltimore, New York, Oklahoma, Louisiana, and various parts of the United States.

Like other ethnic groups, the Africans seemed to have settled and formed a community, and they seemed to have found the need to educate their children in the culture of their people. Most of them occupy strategic positions in the city's work force. They have their own businesses, and their children add to the rising percentage of African Americans in American schools.

Fortunately, multicultural education has taken the center stage in America's educational system, and it has become a very predominant issue in education. Curriculum makers in America are finding ways of revamping school curriculum to accommodate all the cultures represented in the United States schools and to meet the needs and expectations of the students, believing that a people's culture has so much to do with the way they view the world. Therefore to understand the children, one had to understand their culture.

As the purpose of this study was to examine the culture of the African immigrants in America, their struggles, challenges, and triumphs, it was necessary to use a method of data analysis that would permit concepts to emerge from the analysis of data collected in the field. I first made a preliminary reconstructive analysis of the primary data collected during observations, interpreting the interactions from the data for their possible meanings.

Meanings reconstructed from the observations were underscored and enclosed in parenthesis. This method made it easier to revise the interpretations later on and when necessary. The interpretations were also facilitated through member checks.

The findings from the ethnographic analysis articulated the culture of the Africans, their way of life, and their worldview. Since mask carving is the nodal point of this culture, the ethnographic analysis provided adequate background for meaningful interpretation and evaluation of the masks.

What is covered in this study is a set of new perspectives for looking at African culture viewed from the lens of an African, one who has lived in the society he is conducting research, an African cultural –bearer who has had the unique and exceptional privilege of collating data completely immersed in the culture as a full participant for many years, a multicultural educator in America who understands the need for the knowledge and meaningful understanding of all the cultures and peoples that make up America.

As Splinder and Splinder (1965) observe, "descriptions of the thinking and feeling of a people from the inside are not frequent in anthropological literature, for it is difficult for the observer from the outside world to penetrate beyond manifest behavior to the inner patterns of a way of life" (p. vii). Uchendu (1965) adds:

The culture-bearer's point of view presented by a systematic foreign ethnologist who "knows" his natives is not the same as the view presented by a native.... To "live" a culture demands more than a knowledge of its events, systems, and institutions, it requires growing up with these events and being emotionally involved with the cultural values and bias (p. 9).

Nothing in this volume is intended to suggest a detailed uniqueness of the African world. However, every attempt has been made to explore and examine the culture of the vast world of this immigrant African community as it affects their lives in America.

TO THE TEACHER

This book is intended to provide you with a comprehensive view of the culture of the African immigrants in America. Although this volume has long been overdue, it is finally here, and it is timely. The information contained here will allow you to have a global perspective and understanding of the origin of the immigration of this ethnic group and the influence of their presence in the new culture. As you read, you are free to make comparative analysis with your own culture and all the other cultures that make up this great nation.

In the pages that follow, you will learn mostly about the customs and beliefs of the African immigrants, their art, their family values, cultural orientation, their acculturation and enculturation processes, their interface with the dominant culture, and how this transition has affected their family life and belief system.

Some of the customs and beliefs you are about to encounter in this volume may shock you, amaze you, amuse you, or leave you awe-inspired. Some of you may find the whole thing fascinating.

Whatever emotion you come away with as you thumb through these pages, it is my hope that you will hold on to something that is life changing for you---for the better.

As a teacher, I am aware of the need to educate people, especially our children, on the cultures of other peoples. I have, therefore, incorporated some strategies for teaching this culture and the cultures of other ethnic groups.

You really do not need to study the culture of every group before you can begin to teach in a multicultural classroom. The idea is that once you have mastered the strategy for teaching the culture of one ethnic group, you can teach the culture of any ethnic group. This is necessary because, as Takaki (1993) notes, all students in America today need to know much more about the origins and history of the particular cultures which, as Americans, they will encounter during their lives.

My aim is to present the culture of the recent African immigrants to the Americas in a form that informs and teaches the reader. I have done everything I could to make this journey to a strange world as easy as possible without compromising the very essence of cultural discovery. I hope that you will get a lot from this book, and it will change your views about life, yourself, your culture, and the cultures of other peoples of the world.

I must say that this volume has not, in any way, exhausted everything there is to know about this ethnic group. However, I have painstakingly provided information on a culture in transition and the bases for future study on this immigrant group.

To my African immigrant readers, although I have worked hard to include as much information as possible and to make this volume readable, there still exist areas that need to be touched on or further improved. I urge you to send such suggestions and contributions to me care of Mellen Press, and I'll try to incorporate them in future editions. Finally, I want you to enjoy this book.

Darlington I. I. Ndubuike

Acknowledgment

I would like to thank all the groups who allowed me access to the recesses of their ritual grounds and their individual homes, to all whom I interviewed and who sacrificed their time on my behalf, and to all who contributed to the success of this book in one form or another.

I would also like to thank my dear friend, Mr. Lawrence Ukpabi Nwagbara, who proofread the entire manuscript, gave valuable insights, and made recommendations.

Finally, I would like to thank Dr. Fredoline Anunobi of Prairie View A & M University for his insight and suggestions and for accepting to write the foreword to this edition.

CHAPTER 1

I Too Dream America: A Prelude

This evening was a very special evening. The entire Echiele village and its denizens were busy getting ready for the New Yam Festival the next day. The farmers have come home, and the harvest was plentiful. It was time to celebrate the harvest, to present the fruits of our land to *Chukwu Abiama*, God Almighty, and thank Him for a fruitful harvest, long life, and prosperity. It was a time to thank *Ala*, Mother Earth, for fertility, fecundity, and production, for nurturing the land and for tendering the crops.

Mother Earth is believed to be the overseer of all supreme reproductions and responsible for recycling life both in the plant and the animal world. Without her, life would be difficult not just for farmers who attach much sentiment to the land on whom their means of livelihood depend, but also on everyone who feeds from those farmers.

Yam is the crop used for this harvest ritual. It is the king of crops. It represents life itself. In fact, the sanctity of yam is manifested in the belief that yam cannot be stolen either from the farm or from the barn. Anyone caught stealing yam would be stigmatized.

Story was told of a man who got so hungry that he dug up a whole yam from another person's farm. He cut up the whole yam and cooked it, but after eating two pieces, his hunger was gone. It was then that he realized what he had done. The next morning, he was found hanging on a tree in the back of his compound.

The Compounds were cleaned; grounds were swept. The noise of children running to the village stream to fetch water could be heard from the distance. The women had cleaned up the roadways and stream ways.

1

Every child looked forward to this time of the year. It was a time when family members came home from wherever they were, far and near. Train and bus stations were packed full with people waiting to receive their folks.

On the day of the New Yam festival, we would fill every utensil with water. The women would prepare the yams with the hot soup to go with them.

My favorite was to help my uncle kill and prepare the goat. When the food was ready, we would all gather together as family, and Father would take a piece of the yam and a piece of the meat, wave them over our heads, and toss them on the ground, inviting the ancestors and the gods of the land to partake:

Chukwu Abiama,
The Almighty God, eat this.
Our Fathers, eat this.
King of the skies,
This is yours.
All our Ancestors, eat this.
Mother Earth, eat this.
Let the Kite perch;
Let the Eagle perch also.
He who says
Our yams will not mature,
May his yam not sprout.
He who says
Our children will not prosper,
May his never see
The light of day.

He would toss another piece of yam on the ground, and after that, then we would all eat together.

The most exciting part was the dancing at the market square. First, the girls would appear dressed up in their free-flowing short skirts and a piece of cloth across their chests. The rattles on their wrists, ankles, and waists responded rhythmically to their body movement as they swayed and shook the earth with their rhythmic stamping.

The mothers would sing their beautiful songs and dance around the market ground. Their songs told stories of life and motherhood, stories about important events and people, famous native drummers and dancers. They sang songs that told stories about morals and about right and wrong.

I loved to listen to the songs. The farmers would sing while clearing the bushes ready for planting. They would sing while making their mounds or staking their yams. The fishermen would sing about nature and the mysteries under the water. The palm-wine tappers would sing joyful songs about life's refreshing drinks that come from "above."

My friends and I loved to fashion flutes from bamboo stems and trumpets from animal horns. We would sometimes make drums from animal hides and play them during moonlight nights.

I enjoyed all the traditional dances, but the appearance of the masquerade had always been the most spectacular sight and the highlight of the ceremonies. I still remember one such appearance vividly. I was sitting close to my father on this day.

I could sense the heightened anticipation in his eyes. He would smile and nod his head to the rhythm of the intoxicating drums. A bell rang from a distance. Those who were sitting behind taller people stood up, peering at the anticipated direction from which the masquerade would emerge.

Then the sound of the bell became closer and closer; then it became very loud. The masquerade appeared, jumping, stomping, and swirling.

I was awe-struck by his appearance. In fact, he appeared to defy gravity as he swirled and stumped. The colorful rustling costumes, the awe-inspiring mask, the dangling bells and all the chiming, ringing, and clanking accentuated the gestures of his movement. Other elders stood up and joined in the dancing. My father waived his walking stick in the air in total jubilation. I was too afraid to dance. I simply held on tightly to my father's flowing robe as I peered from the corner.

I enjoyed the *Nwanyiotulaukwu* (The Woman with the Big Bottom) masquerade. There were two of them. The "female" appeared first and entertained, but as soon as she was told that "her husband" was coming, she would quickly "sneak" out from behind the crowd. It was fun.

We would also visit other neighboring clans to witness their masquerade performances. My favorites were the *Ajonkwu* of Ovim that sizzled with agility and elasticity, tumbling, jumping, and cutting down palm-fronds and heads of

3

goats with one quick slice of the machete, the sensational *Ebi* of Umuobiala that rattled and chimed and jingled, and the *Ukwom* of Amaibo that swirled and somersaulted endlessly.

But this particular evening was like no other evening. It was an especially different evening. Although it was the eve of the New Yam festival, it nursed a strong promise, an ultimate promise.

The sun was gliding down the sky and dragging home with it the enchantment of the beautiful day. A cool, refreshing breeze was sweeping through my village, whispering of the sun's untimely slumber. The clouds loomed gracefully in sculptured waves over patches of rustling cornrows and faded, tired farmhouses.

My father and I were working in the yam barn behind the big house. We were strengthening the sticks and attaching palm branches and palm leaves to the fence to protect the yams in the barn from invasion by the goats.

My father worked on the outside of the fence, while I worked from within. There were little holes between the fencing sticks, and through these holes, my father would pass the rope to me, and I would pass it round the fencing sticks and then back to him.

Apart from the rustling of the dried palm fronds, the humming of the wind in my ears, the creaking of forest insects, and the singing of birds, all was quiet.

"Onny," Father called, breaking the silence.

"Yes, Father," I answered.

"I want you to go to school and be like Dr. Zik of Africa."

"Did you say school?"

"Yes, Son, I said school."

"And be like Zik?"

"Yes, Son, like Zik. You will go to America and become a Doctor."

Zik was the first president of the Federal Republic of Nigeria. He was a very influential man, and rumor had it that he was so great and famous because he studied in America. He was a very eloquent speaker and handled the English language with the mastery of an educated native speaker. He had so many names, names that echoed his greatness---"Zikism," "Zeeeek," "Azikiwe," and on and on. He was the Owelle of Onitsha, the Zik of Africa.

4

He was my hero. He was born on November 16, and so was I. It was said that people born on this same month and day make great people and great leaders.

So, when Father revealed his thought to me, my young limbs tingled with excitement. I could not contain myself. Perhaps that was the beginning of great things to come. I flung the palm leaves in my hand in the air, leaped with the elasticity of a cat and dashed into the house. My older stepbrother, Nchekwa, was sitting by the fireplace playing his locally made xylophone.

"Nchekwa! Do you know what Father said," I gasped.

"No,' Nchekwa replied.

"Father said I will go to school!" I said.

"School?" Nchekwa asked.

"Yes, brother, school," I said.

"That's good," he replied

"Will you come too?" I asked

"No. You know, I don't want to go to school. I want to be a motor mechanic, but I am glad you are going to school."

"I am so glad," I said, "but I wish you could come too."

Nchekwa began to walk toward her mother's house.

"Father also said that I will go to America and become a doctor," I added.

"You must go, brother. You must go," Nchekwa said, still walking.

Nchekwa and I didn't get along very much. We were always fighting even for very little things. One of my uncles thought that the best way to stop this mess was to give us a chance to just fight and beat each other up. He did. He and my stepmother watched one day as Nchekwa and I clawed it out like Nchanga and Enoma. That was our last fight. From then on, we began to respect each other a little better.

America held so much for everyone. It was called by different names: "The Land of Canaan," "The Land of Milk and Honey," "The Land Where Darkness Never Falls," "The Promised Land," "God's Own Country," and on and on and on.

We were also told that education in America was different. Children went to school free of charge. They did not have to even worry about bringing a long list of books home for their parents to buy. They didn't wear uniforms. They

5

could just dress up in their street clothes. They even ate at school---breakfast and lunch!

They could talk back to the teacher without getting a whipping. That was frightening. It must be a different world indeed. When they came late to school, they would pick up a piece of paper from the office and walk right into the class.

There was a son of the land who went to America to get education. His name was Chukwuma. His "English" name was "Chuk." Some rumored that he changed his name in America, so that the Americans could pronounce it with ease. They could not pronounce *Chukwuma*. We were told that people changed their names or adopted another name in America. A name like Nkem would be "Kim" Ume would be "YouMay." Chike would be "Chyke," and so on.

On the day of Uncle Chukwuma's return home, everybody in the village geared up for his welcome. Shops were closed; every market was closed; stalls were empty, and even schools were closed on this day. The village school brass band supplied the music all day. People lined the streets to behold this "son from yonder." When his motorcade finally arrived, chants rang, banners waved, people cheered, and women sang. It was a day to remember.

Everything about him was completely different. His hair was curlier; his skin was smoother; his clothes were of a better quality than anything anybody had ever seen. When he stepped out of the car, people wanted just to touch his garment. When he smiled, his teeth showed no sign of decay. It was "Pepsodent white," they said.

The elders sat under the canopy. Others sat under the shade of big trees. There were lots of food, music and dancing. Food was plentiful. Basins of rice were served according to family units.

The children also were served a basin of rice with stew and pieces of meat perched scantily all around it. The children couldn't wait to be served. As soon as the basin touched the ground, they pounced on it and on each other with full speed, cupping as much rice as their tiny hands could contain, and munched away. Some of their faces got buried in the basin of rice. Fights erupted here and there as big kids tried to exert their influence.

Parents wished for their children to go to America. They drummed it in their music, hummed it in their tune, sang in their songs, and danced it in their steps. A song by a popular women's dance group explained it all:

6

Ala Bekee mara nma
Ma o di oke onu
O gaghi ahia nwa m iga nmuta
Ma Chi kwe!

This translates:
America is beautiful
But it is expensive
That wouldn't deter my child from going to learn
God willing!

When he spoke, there was no doubt that he had been to America. He was eloquent. He made English language sound easy. His speech was fascinating, interesting, and awe-inspiring.

He told stories of his experiences in America. Food was plentiful in America. For the first time in his life, he said, he was served a whole chicken for dinner.

He recalled his experience one day when a girl in his class said to him, "I'll talk to you later." He stood there for hours waiting for her to come and "talk to him." She actually walked by him and said nothing, like they hadn't met. He later realized that it was an American slang that meant "good-bye."

He blew our little minds when he told us that he would wash dishes in restaurants, just to survive and pay his school fees. He would clean rooms in hotels and make people's beds. He would take two to three jobs and would go from work to school and from school to work.

He also told us that American children went to school for free. Everything was provided for them. They even had big buses that took them to and from school.

It must be a different world, I thought. But why did Uncle Chukwuma have to pay for his? Why did he have to work so hard to get money to pay for his school fees? Why didn't they give him money?

The scariest moment was when he told us that Americans carried guns, and that they could shoot and kill somebody. He told a story of how one of his friends was shot and killed. He was a taxi driver. One of his passengers shot him. He died. They all had to contribute money to send his body home.

I sat there and listened to all he had to say. Most of the things he said were fascinating to me. They fueled my desire to go to America. Some of the things he said were horrible. Sometimes I thought he said all those things to discourage us from going to America. He went there and came home safely, and so would I; I thought to myself.

Before I went to bed that night, I prayed:

"Lord, I thank you. Give me knowledge. Let me get learning. I want to help my father and my sister, my stepbrother and my stepmother and all my family. And help me so that I can go to America. I ask you all this through Jesus Christ our Lord. Amen."

I had gone to bed early that night. Usually, on such moonlight nights, the boys would sit outside the *obi* waiting for dinner to be ready. They would listen to the men talk about brevity and manhood. The girls would help with the cooking, and the mothers would teach them what they needed to know to make their husbands happy.

After dinner, my stepbrothers and I would join the other children in the village square where we would listen to folktales. We would all sit on the sandy ground and listen to old men unfold their beautiful tales.

I was not fond of my mother. For some yet unknown, mysterious reason, Mother and Father parted. They told me that it was not really a divorce. People didn't talk about divorce.

Father told me that marriage was not only a family affair, but also a commitment that involved both the living and the dead. Therefore, both the living and the dead were in it together.

When a man decided to get married, he would invite all his friends and family to witness the ceremony. Kołanut and palm-wine were shared with the living and the dead. In order to get a divorce, my father said, everyone that was present at the wedding must be invited to witness the divorce. Since some of them may be dead or gone, divorce became impossible.

8

Whoever would decide to divorce, against the law of the land, would divorce himself from the protection of the ancestors. In order to avoid the wrath of Mother Earth and the ancestors, men usually did not divorce their wives, they would instead, marry other wives in addition.

I went with the family when my uncle married his third wife. In fact, it was my uncle's first wife who found the girl and recommended her to him. The "Question Askers" had done their job, and everything was fine. There were no stains in the family that would jeopardize the marriage. The marriage was cleared to proceed.

So on the day of the traditional marriage, we all went to our would-be in-laws' house. Almost the whole village went. They presented us with fresh palm wine and kolanut. After we had eaten, my father cleared his throat and told our in-laws our reason for coming.

"The animal we were chasing ran into your house, and we have come in pursuit'" he said. Everyone laughed.

They understood the saying. The girl's father stood up, cleared his throat, and said, "Well, you are all welcome. That animal belongs to me."

He asked one of the boys to call her daughter. When she came, her father asked her if she knew whom the visitors were. She blushed. He then asked her to show him who the chief "hunter" was. They filled up a glass of palm wine, gave it to her, and asked her to give it to the chief "hunter." She did, and everyone cheered. The ceremony went into the wee hours of the morning, after which we took our bride home.

But my own mother left. She thought it was the right thing to do for her life. I still do not know the full story, and I do not think that I ever will. Father died few years ago without telling me the full story; his own side of the story. He said he would, but he did not quite get to it.

My father's death devastated me. I wished he lived to see it all come to pass, to see me go to America, get education, graduate, and become a doctor. I knew he believed in me, and I knew he believed that I would be that which he had dreamed I would be.

My sister and I knew him as both Mother and Father. He was always there for us, a big part of our lives. The words that best described him were kind, gentle, strong, compassionate, and loving. When he died, I knew exactly what I had lost. Something I would never find again. I was sorry. I knew I would miss him. I would miss the stability he represented to me, the inspiration. He was everything to me.

I couldn't really tell what he died of. I knew he had been sick. He had been sick once before. I could remember walking into his room one day. He was covered with thick blanket. He knew it was I, but he didn't say anything. He knew I was there. He raised his right hand and opened his palm. I paced my palm in his. I felt a gentle squeeze. He recovered fully from that sickness. They said it was malaria. I didn't know what this one that took his life was.

Father was kind and treated everyone with respect and dignity. I couldn't possibly understand what went wrong. But Mother left. She left my older sister, Chinasa, whom I fondly and respectfully called and still call China, and me. China was three years old then. I was only six months.

China was a smart girl. She also went to school. She went to college. She was lucky, or should I say, Father was bold. Then, it was not proper to send a female to school. Education was for the boys. The idea was that the girls would eventually get married, leave, and answer someone else's name, but the boys would bear the light of the family.

But China went to school. She eventually went to America. I was at the airport on the day of her departure. It was a very emotional moment for me, a moment of mixed feelings. I would miss her, yet I was glad that she was going to America, a place that I would like to go someday.

As her flight took off, tears ran down my cheeks. I thought about loneliness. She was my mother, my sister, and my friend. I thought about our ordeal right after the civil war ended. The soldiers were snatching every girl that was in sight. We were coming home from the refugee camp. China was dressed in shabby, sun-beaten, weather-damaged, old lady outfit to distract the soldiers. The make-up on her face was sloppily applied.

The journey home was long, in and out of the bushes, through narrow forest paths, and over the hills. At one point, China and I got exhausted. In our hurry and excitement to go home, we had forgotten to take some food with us. Our stomachs growled and pouted, contracted and squeezed.

The bouncing motion of my bicycle as it rolled along the bumpy forest paths, combined with hunger and the deep-seated fear of getting caught, which had kept edging into China's consciousness, had made it all impossible for her to succumb to the urge to rest or drop off to sleep.

As she sat deep in thought on the bicycle carrier, she didn't notice that we had come to a military checkpoint. My bicycle squeaked to a stop, and China immediately realized where we were. I could see her hands starting to shake. Her knees knocked in fear. She was waiting for the worst to happen.

"Who's this person?" one of the soldiers asked, positioning his gun.

"She's my grandmother," I said.

"Good morning, Madam," he said, walking towards China.

China didn't want to say anything for fear of her voice betraying her.

"She's sick, Very sick," I retorted.

"You may go. Give her APC or Aspro," he said.

I was too tired to peddle my bike. My knees were stiff and aching, and I decided to drag the bike along with China on it. About four miles to home, we felt a relief. We could feel the home breeze sifting through our faces. Home at last, we thought.

Still very hungry, we stopped to find something to eat. It was about mid-evening, and most eating places were closed. The "mama put" stands were bare and cold, but I was determined to get some food. We couldn't take any other step without food.

"Wait here while I look for food," I suggested.

China didn't have any choice. I didn't either. We were starving to death, and I had to do something quick.

Desperately, I scampered across the streets searching for an open kiosk.

Thirty minutes later, I came hurrying back. China wasn't there. I searched all over the place, but she was gone. I feared the worse. Where could she be? Did someone take her away? I panicked. We had traveled so far, and just as we got close to home, she was gone.

A passer-by told me that he saw an old lady walking down the road a short while ago. She had waited too long and had gone looking for me. In her anxiety and fear, she had forgotten that she was supposed to walk like an old lady.

One of the crazy soldiers found her and took her to the camp. I cried. Immediately, I decided to go as close to the army camp as I could safely get. I stayed there until it was midnight.

It was very dark, and I was familiar with the camp. I was very tired. The veins in my temple were throbbing. I climbed over fallen logs, crawled across bushes. Creatures filled the darkness with their cries. All the lights in the army camp were out. The only illumination was from the military checkpoint at the main entrance.

Suddenly, I heard a sound of an open door. I froze. A man stepped out into the darkness. I watched him very carefully and silently. He pulled down his shorts and began to water the grass. He walked back in, but didn't shut the door. I ran as quickly but as carefully and silently as I could. As soon as I got to the door, I heard a sob, a subdued sob. It was China. I stood there for a moment wondering what else to do. The sobbing gradually stopped. She had fallen to sleep.

I quietly sneaked in. I didn't want to frighten my sister. I didn't want her to scream in fear. I didn't know what to do. I gently pulled her toe. She jumped like a frightened cat. I cupped her mouth with my hand and called her name. She recognized my voice.

"Come on," I whispered. "Follow me."

I took her by the hand, and we tiptoed outside the room. Then we ran as fast as our tired legs could carry us. We got home safely.

I thought about so many things as I watched her airplane take off that day on her way to America. I thought about what life would be like without her. I thought about her first day in high school. She came home and taught me how to say different words in French, for example *"Bonjour," "Monsieur," "Mademoiselle,"* and so on. She also taught me some French songs. My favorite was the "Au Clair de la lune" song:

Au clair de la lune
Mon ami pierrot
Prete-moi ta plume.
Pour ecrire un mot
Ma chandelle est morte,
Je n'ai plus de feu
Ouvre-moi la porte,

I fell sick the night she left, shivering with high fever. I didn't know what happened, but I heard my father calling out to my uncle to bring a spoon. The next thing I knew, the spoon was stuffed in my mouth between my teeth and my tongue. Less than an hour later, they took off my cloths and covered me with a thick blanket over a hot, steaming pot of *dogoyaro,* leaves from a medicinal tree. Droplets of sweat cascaded down my body. A few hours later, I was given a concoction from this herb to drink. It was worse than bitter.

With little or no money for doctors and with hospitals very far away and expensive, my family made use of many folk medicines and home remedies. These home remedies were believed to "fix" anything from a simple ant bite to a major symptom. My father's cure-all was *Dogoyaro*, especially for malaria and high fever.

The plant was grown on the compound where it could be easily reached and used as need arose. Most people used the *dogoyaro* tree as fence around their compounds.

Father would cut the branches and mix them up with some herb and roots, and he would leave the concoction to ferment for several days. In fact, it could cure anything if one would get past the smell and taste of it. Sometimes I covered my nose to avoid the smell of it. I usually kept an orange handy to suck on right after.

Sloan's Liniment was also Father's multi-purpose medicine. We would chew a cube of sugar soaked in Sloan's Liniment for cough; we would rub Sloan's on our faces to clear up acne, and we would rub it in our hair to clear dandruff. For cuts, scrapes, and minor burns, he would put few drops of the liquid to stop the bleeding.

Father took care of us because Mother left. I asked Mother why she didn't take us with her. She explained that in situations like this, the children belonged to and stayed with their father. There was no dispute about it.

So, we became our father's responsibility, our stepmother's more so. We did not have the best of times, but we survived. We were deprived of so many things, which the other children were given. China would sweep and mop, wipe and clean, and scrub and wash.

One day, as I was coming home from playing football with my friends, I saw China sitting on a pile of dust behind my uncle's house. Her head was sandwiched between her raised knees. Her hands hung loosely on both sides, and her fingers gently caressed the dirt.

I walked up to her and held her shoulder. She looked up. Bitter tears ran down her cheeks. I sat next to her and rested my head on her arms. She put her arm around my shoulder and heaved a sob. I sobbed. We sat there for a long time, in silence.

I grew up not knowing who my "real" mother was. I met her for the first time when I was twelve. Folk tales became a source of emotional relief for me.

Every child looked forward to moonlight nights. Moonlight night was time for stories around the fire. The best stories were told by old men---men who had been warriors in their time, the soon would-be ancestors, the custodians of morality and values, the living libraries of a people who had no books.

They told stories of different kinds---tales of life and death, of good and evil; there were tales of magical adventure, of exploits in war. They told tales about Mother Earth and the gods who rule the land---*Amadioha, Ezemobu, Nneochie, Iyi-Ike, Isi Uzu Amuta,* the gods of the river, of rain, and of thunder and lightning.

Some of their tales caused their audience to tremble with excitement. Some held the listeners spellbound in rapt fascination, especially as the retired warriors unfolded their tales of war and conquest.

They also told comic stories about the trickster, a cunning Tortoise who was always getting his way. He had many names---*Mbediogu, Mbekwu, Mbe Nwa Aniga.* All the stories carry strong morals with them.

I still remember one of those stories very vividly. It was about the tortoise and the pig. The moon was shinning brightly that night as we sat around the compound listening with rapt attention and fascination as Okorie, the oldest man of the village, cleared his throat and began:

"Once upon a time, in the land of Anumanu, there lived a lazy and cunning tortoise named *Mbekwu* who knew the way to trick himself out of every difficulty. While his neighbors cultivated virgin farmlands during planting season, the slothful Tortoise stayed home and depended on feeding from his hardworking friends. He studied all types of smoke and could tell which smoke signified that the food was still cooking and the smoke that meant that the food was ready.

Every day, the tortoise would sit outside and would watch the fume that came out of his neighbors' kitchens. Then he would hurry to where the food seemed ready. He was lucky, too. He had kind and generous neighbors who always invited him to dinner whenever he came around. He would eat and eat and eat until his body filled his shell. Then, he would take the scraps for his wife and son at home to eat.

He played this prank successfully for a long time until he began to run out of luck. All his neighbors had discovered his trick and had learned to ignore him whenever he came to them.

One afternoon, the tortoise went to the pig's house when the pig was eating dinner. The pig disregarded the starving tortoise and didn't invite him to dine with him as usual. The famished tortoise brushed pride aside, stooped down, and began to nibble at the scrap of food that had fallen on the floor while the pig ate.

"Can I ask you a little favor?" said the tortoise, pathetically.

"What is it?" grumbled the pig.

"Can you loan me three pennies till tomorrow," Tortoise begged. "My family and I are starving to death."

"You know something, my children," the wise storyteller said, " a penny at that time could buy dinner for the whole family. That was when the world was blind and the soil was fertile. Now, things have changed!"

He continued:

"My father told me neither to loan money to anyone nor borrow from anyone," replied Pig. "Besides, all I have to my name is six pennies, and I don't intend to part with a penny of it."

"One penny will do," Tortoise begged. "I'll pay you back in five days.

"I know you very well, Tortoise," said Pig. "You are very cunning and crafty. You reap where you did not sow."

"Believe me," swore Tortoise, "I've changed. I'll pay you within five days. I promise."
The soft-hearted Pig loaned Tortoise two pennies.

"Thank you, my friend," Tortoise said, smiling. "A friend in need is a friend indeed."

On his way home, Tortoise laughed until his ribs were sore. He had fooled Mr. Pig.

The fifth day, Mr. Pig went to Tortoise's house to collect his money. The sneaky Tortoise saw Mr. Pig from a distance and ran into the house.

"Son!" Tortoise screamed. "Tell that fat old pig that I went to his house."

Tortoise hid himself under the bed. Soon, his creditor arrived.

"Where is your father?" asked Mr. Pig.

"He told me he was going to your house." Little Tortoise lied.

"I've just left my house. He wasn't there," replied Mr. Pig.

"Perhaps you crossed each other's path," Little Tortoise said.

As soon as the pig left, Tortoise crawled out from under the bed. He and his son laughed and laughed and laughed. The next day, Tortoise saw Mr. Pig coming. He hurriedly ran into the house and hid himself behind the door. In his haste, he didn't notice that his toes were sticking out from under the door.

"Where's your father?" asked Mr. Pig.

"He's not here," said little Tortoise.

Mr. Pig looked down and saw Tortoise's toes sticking out. Upset and aware of Tortoise's deceit, he purposely leaned hard on the door, pressing the bolt hard on tortoise's ribs.

"You little demon!" Mr. Pig cursed. "Tell your father to take his toes with him when next he goes out.

As soon as Mr. Pig left, Tortoise staggered out from behind the door holding his chest.

"That fat, ugly pig almost squeezed me to death with that door knob." Tortoise gasped.

Soon, the Pig returns, this time with anger and vengeance. Tortoise saw him fuming.

"Take this tobacco and grind it on that stone," said Tortoise to his wife. "Tell Mr. Pig that I'm not home."

"But I don't have a grinding stone," replied Tortoise's wife.

"Don't worry," said Tortoise. "I'll be the grinding stone."

Tortoise slid his head, hands, and legs into his shell, and his wife used him as the grinding stone. Soon, the pig arrived.

"Where's your husband?" asked Mr. Pig.

"He's not here." Replied Tortoise's wife.

"That cunning, ugly devil!" Mr. Pig cursed. "I thought he had changed. He is still the same old cheat. I'll wait for him this time."

"But he won't be home till late," said Little Tortoise.

"Shut up! You little brat," snapped Mr. Pig. "I've had enough of you. Your lazy father must pay me today, or I'll beat the last breath out of him."

Mr. Pig waited and waited and waited, but Tortoise didn't come home. Little Tortoise began to giggle. His mother joined in. Mr. Pig knew that they were making fun of him. He boiled and blazed with furry. The more they laughed, the more enraged he became.

Mr. Pig decided that he had had enough of that. He sprang up from the chair, snatched the grinding stone from Tortoise's wife, and flung it in the air. The stone fell into the mud. Little Tortoise and his mother began to scream.

Meanwhile, Tortoise had sneaked out of the mud and gone to a nearby stream where he washed himself clean. He came home and saw his family crying.

"What's the matter?" inquired Tortoise.

"Mr. Pig threw away my grinding stone," Tortoise wife complained.

"Why did you throw away my wife's grinding stone?" Tortoise asked Mr. Pig. "She didn't owe you any money. She did nothing to you!"

The angry pig refused to answer. His chest pounded with anger and hate.

"I'll not pay you until you find my wife's grinding stone," Tortoise gruffed.

Mr. Pig thought he knew the exact spot where the grinding stone had fallen into the mud, so he went to look for it. He grubbed and grubbed, but there was no trace of the stone. He began to sniff the mud for a scent of tobacco, which he hoped, would lead to the discovery of the grinding stone.

To this very day, the pig is still sniffing and grubbing the mud in search of Tortoise's grinding stone."

Every time I see a pig or a tortoise, this story immediately comes to mind, but my favorite tales were those about motherless children who found favor with benevolent spirits. I drew my courage and inspiration from them.

So, when Father told me that I would be going to school, I felt the dawning of a bright future. The old men were wise. Their stories were true. Perhaps those benevolent spirits had found me. These thoughts fell on my ears like phrases of divine music.

But this particular night was different. The sun had crept behind the clouds and the moon had risen in its place. The flickering lamplight from the "Obi" (central house) cast a quiet glow over the compound. It was a perfect night for storytelling, but my desire to get learning outweighed any interest in the moonlight night entertainment.

The nights suddenly became longer. I woke up many times during the night and peeked outside to see if the day had dawned. I opened one eye slowly. It was still dark outside. I squeezed both eyes tightly shut as if that would squeeze away the darkness.

Finally, Monday came, and I was very happy. I was excited about my new slate and pencil, and especially about my school uniform of white shirt and brown khaki shorts. I was particularly excited about this rare opportunity of going to school, of learning English, of going to America to become a doctor, and of being like my idol, Dr. Zik.

Early that next morning, before the first streaks of daylight silvered the sky, I was ready for school. I ran across to my father's "obi". The door of the "obi" was half open. The scent of ingredients for evocation permeated the air. The rays of light pouring from the hurricane lamp sitting on the high window of the room silhouetted the figure at the corner of the room. Father was offering his early morning sacrifice and prayers, but today was a very special one. His son was going to school.

I tiptoed into the room. I did not want to disturb the silence, which at that moment was sacred, a hymn to divinity, a prelude to holiness. In that silent state, the spirit suppressed all verbal expression and became a fertile ground for the advent of the superhuman. It permeated the total being of my father that morning as he evoked the spirit of the ancestors.

I watched with silent admiration as my father performed this ritual. He picked up one kolanut, broke it, and tossed some of the pieces on his Ikenga. Then he ate a piece of it, which he had dipped into a mixture of pepper, peanut, and fresh palm oil.

My father told me a lot about kolanut. It was like no other nut. It was the nodal point of all rituals. No ritual is complete without it. It represented the "Duity," the original concept of our traditional religion. It was a symbol of goodwill and well-being, a means of communication with the ancestors and with the cosmic rhythm.

Then, he picked up a calabash of palm-wine and poured some of the contents into a long calabash gourd. He began to speak. There was nobody else in the room at that time. He hadn't noticed that I was there. He must then be speaking to some invisible presence. He knelt beside the shrine in silence. On other occasions, he would invite them to eat kolanut and to drink palm-wine. He would ask for peace, protection, strength, long-life, and prosperity. Today, he must be asking for divine favor on my behalf, for knowledge, wisdom, guidance, protection, and care.

Palm-wine was known as the traditional beverage. It came from palm tree. Individuals owned these trees, and they either tapped the wine themselves or had someone do it for them. Palm-wine contained yeast, they said, and it was served to nursing mothers. It was believed to aid in the formation of breast milk.

During market days, palm wine was not sold. It was given freely to all who visited. On certain market days, people would go in groups from one tapper to another for free drinks.

This particular morning was different. His son was going to school. It was the beginning of things to come---good things!

My father and I shared a lot of secrets. He told me of his triumphs and defeats. He told of his joys and sorrows, his frustrations and grief.

He fought during World War II. He would always tell about the Hitler war, and his experiences in Burma. He would get excited and begin to march around the compound like a soldier. He would use any stick for a raffle. He would call out the commands and would execute them.

"Attention!"
"Present...Arm!"
"Right...Turn!"
"By the Left, mark time!
"Left, Right, Left, Right!"

As I stood there quietly and watched him, I could feel his tenacity, his courage. I could still hear him say, "Nothing comes easy, Son. You must continue to persevere."

Few moments later, Father stood up, placed his hands on my head and said, "The spirit of our fore-fathers will guide you. *Chukwu Abiama* will lead you. Go, and do not be afraid."

Suddenly, from the distance, the sound of the *Ikoro* bellowed. It was so loud and clear that one could decipher the message it bore.

Ikoro was a wooden drum used to disseminate information to every part of the village. Once it began to speak, every one was quiet. Father stopped momentarily. It wasn't a bad message, so Father was calm. The last time the *ikoro* sounded, the message was not too good. It was about the death of Okorie, the oldest man in the village, the wise storyteller.

Father rubbed his finger across my eyes and washed my face with water stored in a calabash. He shook my hand and embraced me.

I set off for the seven-mile walk to school. Dry leaves crushed beneath my footsteps as I trod steadily barefoot down the bush path. About half a mile to school, I heard the school bell ring.

It was eight O'clock. I was late on my first day of school. I had been told about the teachers' *koboko*, a cane fashioned from tough animal leather. It was the major disciplinary tool for all types of offences. The popular adage at that time was "Save the whip and spoil the child." I did not want to start my first day with lashes on my back and buttocks.

I heard scary stories about the gate man, Mr. Archibong. He was said to have his heart in the back of his chest. That was how mean and wicked he was. He was only a gate man, but he manhandled children, especially the latecomers. I didn't want to run into him at all. His knuckles were stiff and crooked, perhaps from so much whipping. He would curse sometimes in his native dialect, especially when he did not want the children to understand, but they could tell it was bad. Children called him "yam," because he had big calves, seemingly out of proportion.

Well, I secured my slate tightly under my left arm and flung myself into the air like a Zen arrow flying through the forest. I ran like a well-lubricated paddlewheel, swift and sure. My thin arms cut through the air in rapid, even strokes. The cool morning breeze sifted through my hair.

"Hey! Come here." A short man with thick moustache and scanty goatee snapped as I tried to sneak my way across the barbed wire fence. It was Mr. Wuru.

I snapped to attention like a marionette manipulated by some unseen hand. There were about ten others on the ground waiting to receive the *koboko*. I sat down among them. My young mind dwelt on the many stories about teachers and their canes.

"Wuru," the teacher said.

The boys bent down touching their toes with the tip of their fingers. Every one of them was shaking like a leaf brushed by a passing wind.

In fact, the teacher was a popular figure in the school and neighboring villages, a brusque blustery man with cheery disposition and an earthy village-style sense of humor. He spoke the smattering of five languages, but handled only his tribal tongue with any degree of fluency.

He always wore colorful attire, which echoed the varied tropical foliage that seemed as a perennial backdrop to village life. Everyone called him Mr. Wuru. His real name was Kofi Kwame. His nickname was derived from his method of discipline.

In fact, every teacher used the *koboko*, but not in the style of Mr. Wuru. Parents brought their recalcitrant and disobedient children to teachers for discipline. Of course, children would not want to offend their parents to the point where they would be referred to Mr. Wuru.

So, when I watched the other children receive Mr. Wuru's *koboko*, needless to say that my heart beat three hundred times in a split second. I propped on my elbows with my chin in my hand. When it got to my turn, I froze with fear.

"Wuru," the teacher said.

I bent over, and, like the clap of thunder, the whip cracked on my back and buttocks five times in quick succession. I let out a high-pitched scream that tore through the still morning air. I rubbed my buttocks and tears came streaming down my cheeks.

"Go over there," Mr. Wuru said, pointing to the open field.

22

I picked up my slate with one hand, rubbed my buttocks with the other, and staggered to the field in front of the school building where all the teachers and pupils stood. It was the morning routine to have all the children inspected for cleanliness.

"School, hands up!" shouted one of the teachers. He was the teacher on duty that morning.

All hands went up in the air.

"Down!"

"Up!"

"Down!"

"Up!"

"Clap one!"

All the children clapped above their heads.

"Clap two!"

"School, clap three!"

"Hands down!"

"Hands on your neighbor's shoulders---place!"

We all executed the command, forming three straight lines with an arm length space between us.

"Hands down!"

"Right turn!"

"Hands in front--- stretch!"

We stretched out our hands in front of us.

"I-N-S-P-E-C-T-I-O-N!" he finally roared.

My fingernails were as long as the tiger's. I did not know that I was supposed to cut them, especially on Mondays, the inspection days. No one told me. Perhaps it was one of those things that one has to find out. I found out.

There was one teacher to a line. Mr. Wuru was assigned to inspect my line. I almost wet my shorts when I saw Mr. Wuru with his *koboko*. The boy standing beside me had a bushy hair, and the *koboko* descended on his head twice. His face broke into a distasteful, toothless grin.

I realized what was coming my way. I could almost hear my knees knocking in fear. My hair was neither cut nor combed. My fingernails were long and dirty. The *koboko* cracked the air and the lash fell across my head and my back.

"Next time, cut your hair, Bushman," Mr. Wuru said, still flogging.

"Yes, Sir," I answered painfully, bouncing up and down like a ping-pong ball.

One other boy standing beside me giggled.

"Short up!" I snapped.

"ATTEN-TION!" the teacher on duty cried out.

"By the left, mark time. Left, right, left, right. Forward---march!"

The children began to sing a song. It was a familiar tune because I had heard school children sing it at home several times:

I am H-A-P-P-Y
I am H-A-P-P-Y
I know
I'm sure
That I am H-A-P-P-Y.

The drums beat, and the flutes sang. I marched on happily despite the beating I had received earlier. My excitement outweighed the pains I felt from the bruises I sustained from the *koboko*.

To have the opportunity to go to school was an excitement by itself; not everyone had the opportunity. To me, it was the ultimate promise. The *koboko* was a part of going to school, and I knew it from the start.

I stretched my hands as far as they could go--- forward, backward, forward, backward, forward---alternately to the intoxicating, intricate rhythm of the village school brass band. Once in a while, my feet lost the pace, and I watched the other children's steps in order to fall back in rhythm. I even made up my own lyrics to go with the music of the marching band:

Kpowa teacher nde one
Ota ntanta
Kpowa teacher nde two
Ota ntanta

24

Jikerewenu nde uka
Father na-abia

I marched on and on, looking to my sides at intervals to see if any one noticed how proud I was to be a pupil of St. Celina's Elementary School. Rivulets of hot salty sweat streamed down my face and burned when a few of the droplets eased their way into the tiny cuts made by Mr. Wuru's *koboko*. I really didn't feel the hurt that much. I was happy to be in school.

One could see in my face the dawn of a new life as I and the other children stood in the school hall listening to the headmaster who welcomed us to school. We sang some songs that morning. Most of them were new to me. I knew some of them. I heard the other kids sing them when they returned from school. When they began to sing one of my favorites, I joined in:

O Dina, osisi mango
　　O Dina
O Dina, osisi mango
　　O Dina
I na-eri jakpu?
　　Dina
I na-eri alibo?
　　Dina
I makwa kosi ato?
　　Dina

We clapped and stumped and sang. Every child loved to sing. The songs, the singing, and the dancing expressed different feelings---feelings of hope, joy, sorrow, grief, and loneliness.

Each day began with prayers. Above the assembly hall was a big round plaque on which was inscribed, "Cleanliness is next to Godliness." The assistant principal drew our attention to it and told us that it was the school's motto. He read it to us, and we repeated after him. "What's a motto?" I asked myself. He must have read my mind because he explained to us what that meant. I wondered

25

if that was why we had to go through such rigorous inspection every Monday morning.

Before we prayed, we sang songs from the *"Songs of Praise"* hymnal. They were all beautiful songs, but the one that stuck with me was *"Pass me not O gentle Savior."* For some reason, I felt very secure and confident after the hymn.

While we closed our eyes to pray, I repeated my prayer from the previous night. I was ready.

Soon after, the assistant to the headmaster grouped us in classes. My teacher was Mr. Wuru. Bashuru was appointed the class monitor. His main responsibilities included alerting the class of Mr. Wuru's entry, to write names of noisemakers, to arrange the teacher's desk, and to carry home his books, class register, and his stool.

As the class monitor, Mr. Wuru allowed him to use pen and ink. The pen was a wooden type with nib. To write, one had to dip the nib into a bottle of ink.

Not everyone was allowed to write with pen and ink. It was a special privilege for those whose penmanship was exemplary. Some were stuck with pencil for the entire year.

I was excited when Mr. Wuru cleared me to use pen and ink. My favorite ink color was blue. It looked beautiful on paper, but Mr. Wuru insisted that we used the blue-black ink.

The first time I used ink, I was so proud. I purposely smeared some on my white shirt, so that people who saw me would know that I was a scholar, and that I had been approved to use pen and ink---not pencil. It was a proud feeling.

Everyone knew that not many parents could afford to send their children to school. Nothing was free, from primary school to college. One had to pay for everything---pencil, ruler, slate, chalk, books, eraser, and in fact, everything, not to mention the almighty tuition.

There were times when Father could not come up with the school fees in time, and I was asked to go home until I brought my money. There were many others who shared the same fate. Sometimes, a crack of the whip on our backs heralded our departure. It was our fault, it seemed, that our parents couldn't afford to pay the fees on time.

There were some lucky children who were never sent home for their fathers' inability to pay their school fees, but I was glad to be me. I was even thankful that I could go to school with the sons of the wealthy.

So, when they would send us out of the class, I would go home and run straight to the farm where Father was working. I would help him till the ground, cut the bushes, plant the seeds, or stake the yams.

Going to the farm with Father was fun. He would not let us go everyday, but when he did allow us to go with him, he would make sure that we had our favorite farm food---roasted yam with red palm oil and fresh red and green paper.

The yam was roasted in the open fire made with logs of wood. When done, Father would scrape off the burnt surface with knife and cut them in slices. He would then put some fresh red palm oil in a ceramic bowl, cut green and red pepper into tiny slices, and mix them with the palm oil. We would sit together under a shed and eat. Sometimes the yam would be very hot, and we would have to keep our mouths open for a little while to let some of the heat out before we began to chew.

After eating, we would rest for a while before going back to work. Most of the time, after the food, I did nothing else but run around in the farm chasing one grasshopper or another.

My favorite was chasing *igrube,* a giant grasshopper. Sometimes the chase would lead to an unpredictable adventure into the heart of the woods, away from the sounds of human. One could easily get lost in this venture. The *igrube* would fly and perch at very short intervals, enticing its predator.

I got lost several times, and Father would call out loud. I would follow his big voice back to where he was. I would then gather firewood and tie them up in bundles for sale. Sometimes, I tilled others' farms for money.

My friends, Chinyere and Chijioke, and I had a wonderful time growing up together. We belonged to the Ochonma Age Grade. Boys were admitted into this age group after having successfully completed a test of manhood.

The older age group administered the test. They took turns whipping us to see who would cry. Whoever cried or shed tears was disqualified. He would wait until the next induction season.

They emptied buckets of water on us and called us all types of names. They told us it was a test of endurance, to prove our readiness to face the challenges of manhood. We all made it successfully the first time, and we were proud of ourselves.

We also went bird hunting in the bushes together. We would hide under the trees and wait for the birds to perch. We would shoot them down with our tight catapults--- a two-pronged wooden hunting tool fashioned with rubber and leather and shot with a pebble.

We also set traps for rabbits and other rodents. We even fashioned fish traps and used them to catch fish. We would lower the fish traps in the river at night. The following morning, we would return to retrieve the fish in them.

So, when I was sent home from school, my friends and I would team up to work. We would take turns working for one person every day. Eventually, my fees added up, and I was glad to go back to school. It was not once; it was not twice.

Mr. Wuru was fond of long words. People said he was a very learned man. His favorite hobby was copying jaw-breaking words from his Chambers Dictionary and baffling the children with them. Some of those words echoed in my childhood memory---"Tintinnabulation," "Cacophony," "Auditory hallucination."

I learned some big words too and how to spell them. My first big word was "*Shekelekebangoshay*." I learned how to spell it in syllable. I didn't know what that word meant. It was a long popular word among the students, and I could spell it. That was all that mattered.

As Mr. Wuru walked into the classroom, Bashuru struck his stick three times on the desk. Everyone stood up.

"Good morning, Sir!" Everyone greeted in unison.

"Good morning, class. Please be seated," he said, walking to his desk.

It had always been that way. All the children must sit still in their seats ready to welcome the teacher. No one dared to make a sound. The class monitor would write your name down on a piece of paper if you dared.

When Mr. Wuru asked us to sit down, we all sat down in our desks, looking expectantly on the chalkboard. This ritual of greeting the teacher was done two times a day, one in the morning and one in the afternoon after long recess.

Recess time was a fun time. It was time for free play. We would gather in little groups to do our own things. Some played football; some ran races, and others just watched. I loved to do the *Sanga* dance:

Sanga, Sanga
   E-hei
Sanga, Sanga
   E-hei
Sanga Bele Bele
   E-hei Belebe Sanga, E-hei!

We would throw our legs forward and backwards alternately to the rhythm. Then at *"Belebe Sanga"* we would swirl around twice, and so on.

The girls played separately in their groups. They clapped and ran around the circle. Sometimes I would stop and watch them.

I was not really watching all of them. I had special interest on one of them. Her name was Vaku. Her parents were from Togo. Her father was the stationmaster at the local Railway Station.

Vaku was beautiful and slender built. She had dark eyes and a long neck. Her hair was always combed and dressed with multicolored beads.

She didn't like me. Mr. Wuru assigned her a desk close to mine, but she would always move her desk away from mine. She would refuse to speak to me.

But today at recess, my eyes were on her all through. She was the best dancer in the group. One time, her eyes met mine, and I waved at her. She blushed and ran away. I wasn't too sure what she was thinking about at the time. I knew she didn't like me, but I liked her a lot.

On our way back to the classroom, I felt a slight pinch on my neck. I turned around and saw her trying to hide behind one of her friends. Perhaps she liked me too, I thought.

After school that day, she and I walked home together. We became good friends from then on.

At the end of recess, everyone would come in sweating. We would use our books to fan off the heat. Some used their clothes to wipe off the sweat.

As we sat down waiting, Mr. Wuru brought out a big, long book with hard cover. It was the class register. Everyone's name was supposed to be on it.

"My name is Mr. Kofi, and I am your teacher," Mr. Wuru said, sitting on the edge of his table with his legs crossed. He took out a red pen from the side pocket of his shirt. There were about five pens of different colors clipped to that shirt pocket.

"Bashuru Ashuru"

"Present Sir"

"Vaku Kwame"

"Present Sir"

"Aliku Ambrose"

"Present Sir"

"Ebube Dike"

"Present Sir"

"Emeka Nwankwo"

"Present Sir"

"Ogbenyealu David"

"Present Sir"

He went on and on until he had called everyone's name, but my name was not on Mr. Wuru's roll book. He asked me to see him after school. I was scared to death. I didn't know why my name was not there. I became very nervous.

"We will learn English today," Mr. Wuru said, spelling out the word "English" on the chalkboard.

I was glad. English was my ticket and gateway to America, and I was going to begin my learning with it.

"Repeat after me," said the teacher, pointing to a visual aid on the corner of the chalkboard.

TEACHER:	A man
CLASS:	A man
TEACHER:	A pan
CLASS:	A pan

30

TEACHER:	A man and a pan
CLASS:	A man and a pan
TEACHER:	A pan and a man
CLASS:	A pan and a man
TEACHER:	He is a man
CLASS:	He is a man
TEACHER:	It is a pan
CLASS:	It is a pan
TEACHER:	(Pointing at a picture of a pan) Is this a man?
CLASS:	No, it is a pan.
TEACHER:	(Pointing at a picture of a man) Is this a pan?
CLASS:	No, it is a man.
TEACHER:	Very good! Now, listen very carefully. I am standing up. What am I doing? Your response will be, "You are standing up." Now, what am I doing?
CLASS:	You are standing up.
TEACHER:	Again
CLASS	You are standing up.
TEACHER:	Again.
CLASS:	You are standing up.
TEACHER:	Very, very good!

"What is your name?" Mr. Wuru said, pointing at me.

"My name is Onny, I answered.

"Good, Onny, stand up," Mr. Wuru said.

I gradually stood up. Learning English was all right, but not when I stood up for all eyes to watch me.

"What are you doing?" asked Mr. Wuru.

"You are standing up," I responded faintly.

"What are you, you doing?" Mr. Wuru asked again, pointing at me.

"You are standing up," I responded, gulping in my words like beads of dark water.

"No, no, no, no, no!" yelled Mr. Wuru, impatiently. "What are you, I mean you, doing?"

31

I stood very confused. My fingers fidgeted at the sides of my brown khaki shorts. I looked down to my right, listening for a whisper from Wiley, a boy sitting next to me. Wiley would not dare to make a sound. Mr. Wuru was right there.

Hands were raised up around me. I felt more and more nervous, confused, and foolish. I could feel my stomach turn over, slowly, gradually, a porpoise in deep water. I gave up the very attempt to answer.

Mr. Wuru turned to the class and pointed to Isaka, another boy sitting beside me.

"Stand up," Mr. Wuru said. "What are you doing?"

"I am standing up," Isaka answered.

"Good!" said Mr. Wuru. "Now, Onny, what is he doing?"

"I am standing up," I said, hoping that I had said it right that time.

The class giggled.

"Class, what is he doing?" Mr. Wuru asked the whole class.

One could tell from the tone of his voice that he was getting frustrated.

"You are standing up," the class sang in chorus.

"No, no, no, no, no!" cried Mr. Wuru, holding his head in his hands. "I am asking... What is he, he, I mean he, doing?" pointing at the boy still standing up. His eyes bulged with anger.

The class was confused, nervous, and afraid and quietly sang, "You are standing up."

"This is the worst class I've ever taught. Look here, you silly, chicken heads. How long will it take you to understand simple things?" Mr. Wuru said, boiling with rage. "You all have a problem---a very big problem. You are not paying attention at all. Go home and practice it. If I come tomorrow and find that you make a single mistake, I will punish you severely. In fact, there will be no recess tomorrow until you get it right---every single one of you. Today, you may go for free play." Mr. Wuru left.

Angry at my poor performance, I now tried to re-establish myself by telling the other children what they ought to have answered, "He is standing up."

"Be quiet!" shouted Toby. "Why did you not say so when the teacher asked you, if you are that clever?"

32

Everybody in the school was afraid of Toby. He was very muscular and appeared older than everyone else in the class. He beat up people for nothing. When he pinned you down, he wouldn't let go until you called him "Dad" or "Uncle" or whatever else he wanted to be called.

Everybody wanted to be his friend or tried to be on his good side. I remained quiet as he barked at me.

The rest of the day was not as bad as the beginning. Arithmetic, Nature Study and other subjects were better. I was not as nervous as I was earlier in the day. Perhaps I had begun to get used to Mr. Wuru and his teaching method.

We learned a lot of songs and poems. My favorite was an English song about Spring Time:

> *Good morrow to you Spring Time*
> *Good morrow Daffodils.*
> *Good morrow dainty, Primrose that freckled the tiny hills.*
> *The cows are on the meadow grass*
> *The sheep, the lamb can sleep.*
> *Good morrow to you, Spring Time*
>
> Good morrow Daffodils!

Mr. Wuru told us that snow fell during the winter in America. I wondered what that would look like. I wondered about "White Christmas," and about Santa Claus and his red-nosed reindeer. I wondered about Frosty, the Snow Man. I longed to play with him.

I loved our reading book. It had many fascinating stories. There was a story about *Nchanga* and *Enoma*, the sun and the moon that got into a physical combat to gain supremacy. We also read about *Thur*, the god of thunder. When he traveled in the heavens, his chariot rumbled in the sky above, creating claps of thunder below.

Mr. Wuru taught us many songs. The *linen* song was one of my favorites. We would simulate the washing of linens in a basin as we sang the song.

We are washing, washing
Linens.
We are washing linens clean.
This way---
Tralala
That way---
Tralala
This way---
Tralala
That way---
1, 2, 3.

Our English book had a lot of poems too. Mr. Wuru would read them aloud to us and asked us to repeat after him. He would ask us to memorize the verses for individual recitation.

I chose the poem about frogs and school. When it came my turn to recite, I began:

Twenty frogeyes went to school
Down beside a rushing pool
Twenty little coats of green
Twenty vests all white and clean
Master bullfrog grave and stern
Called the frogeyes in their turn
Taught them how to nobly thrive
Likewise how to leap and dive.

Mr. Wuru was so impressed. The class clapped and clapped. I bowed with pride and fulfillment. School was good indeed. Learning English wasn't bad after all.

The school bell rang. It was time for compound work. We all took off our shirts and picked up our long machete. The boys were assigned to cut the grass all around the school compound, while the girls swept and trimmed the sidewalk.

My class was assigned to work on the flowerbeds. We uprooted the weeds, clawed the soil, and poured manure on the flowerbeds. There could have been more than twenty of those flowerbeds around the school.

34

The school day ended well. I was so happy that I could go to school; that I could actually do those things that I watched other children do while I was at home. I cried tears of joy.

On my way home, I recited the morning English lesson. I even made a song of it. It was not a meaningful song, but it was like an opening on a wall through which I saw in the distance a strange but fascinating new world, and I was happy.

When I got home, I rehearsed the lesson with everybody---my father, my sister, my stepbrothers, and especially my older stepbrother, Nchekwa. My father was particularly happy. He gave me a big hug and called me his American boy.

That night was particularly special. The birds sang their lullaby to the tired, drowsy day. The insects creaked; the wind hummed; the leaves danced, and my heart beat to the intricate rhythm of this inimitable blend of nature's own musical ensemble. Through an open window, I could see the leaves of plantain plants wave and sway in an occasional breeze, lifting their green foliage as if to extend a greeting.

I lay down on my bamboo bed and thought about school and learning. I fell asleep and dreamed about life and education in America.

CHAPTER 2

"Cry the Beloved Continent"

Like the little boy, Onny, whom we met in Chapter I, every African, young and old alike, dreams of coming to America. This dream is intensified by the deplorable political, economic, and social situation of the continent.

Onny's father originally desired for him to go to America, get education, and return home to help the family. Today, for many Africans, there is no "home" to return to.

Parents and relatives even encourage their loved ones to stay in America. War, injustice, poverty, tyranny, oppression, depression, harsh economic conditions, hate, envy, and intense conflicts have added more miles on the distance that separates them from their motherland; the land of their birth; the land they left behind.

Africa is the second largest continent in the world and is a wonderfully rich mix of peoples, languages, and customs. It is a continent blessed with abundant human and natural resources. Unfortunately, the continent has suffered tremendous agony in the hands of people, both foreign and domestic.

As a continent, Africa has cried in the hands of foreign oppressors. Today, this Cradle of Civilization has continued to cry in the hands of her own children, the ruthless sadists, the rulers of the continent who have set out to usurp power and amass wealth to the detriment of the masses. These rulers have plunged the continent into political turmoil, social upheaval, and economic chaos.

They invest their countries' money in the purchase of weapons to kill their own people, fueling internal uprisings and instigating conflicts and wars. The unfortunate outcomes of these heinous practices include the conflict between the Hutus and the Tutsis of Burundi, the conflict between the Igbo and the Hausa of

37

Nigeria, the Ethiopian and Eritrean squabbles, and the tension that exists between the Rebels in Sierra Leone and the people of Congo. The list could go on and on.

The cry is loud and clear, and many Africans at home and abroad are echoing this bitter sentiment and crying bitter tears. Umez (2001) points out that the reason for this political disaster was that the minds of 90 percent of these African leaders have been poisoned by colonial mentality, inferiority complex, and mental slavery, which have caused them to think that the current mass exodus of so many Africans to other continents is normal.

The continent's manpower was dealt a deathblow by slave trade and colonization. The continent has suffered untold hardship in the hands of its leaders, and has moaned in the face of tribal unrests and civil wars. Its people are looking for ways to mend broken fences and heal old wounds and ways to bring peace and prosperity back to the land and its people, but their plea have seemed to fall on deaf ears.

Things have continued to fall apart, and people are deserting, searching for peace, freedom, and prosperity in foreign lands. The sad part is that about 88 percent of those Africans who migrate to America are the cream of the crop, with high school education or higher (Speer, 1994). The cry is loud and clear!

According to the data from the United States Immigration and Naturalization Service, more than at any time since World War 1, the United States population increase is driven by the immigration of different peoples from different countries and cultures (Friedman, 1998), and this data, to a great extent, include the immigrants from Africa.

During slavery years, millions of thousands of Africans were forcefully shipped to America to work the plantations. Since the end of the years of forced sequestration of Africans from Africa to America, only a small number of Africans have been able to come to the United States. For example, immigration records show that from 1820 to 1993, only 418,000 African immigrants were allowed to enter the United States (Wynn, 1995). Two-thirds of all African immigrants currently in the United States arrived after 1980 (Brandon, 1997).

38

Speer (1995) noted that only one willing African was recorded by the Immigration and Naturalization Service to have entered the United States in 1820, and the number increased to sixteen all through the decade and continued to climb until the 1960s. From 1965, a new wave of African immigration to America began. As N'Diaye (1997) noted, this was perhaps due to the new immigration legislation that was enacted in the United States which eliminated the system of national quotas for the Western hemisphere and replaced it with an overall limit of 120,000 immigrants.

Several reasons account for the relative fewness of the number of Africans in America prior to 1965. According to Unger (1995), one of the reasons was the difficulty for many Africans in obtaining immigrant visas to the United States. Another strong reason was that only few African families could afford to pay their children's or relation's way to the United States. Also, to many Africans and their families, America was a distant land, a land that could only be imagined or seen in dreams.

The newest wave of immigration was sparked by economic and political upheavals and was fueled by the Immigration Reform Act of 1986, which made it easier for African immigrants to obtain permanent status and remain in the United States. The introduction of the Diversity Visa program by the United States Immigration and Naturalization Services brought in many more Africans to America.

As their number increases, they have begun to identify themselves as one group and have found the need to participate in cultural activities, programs, and conferences together in order to identify their collective presence in the larger community. As N'Diaye (1997) puts it, they "describe a development of consciousness of themselves as members of an ethnic group, of a larger national community, of Africa as a whole, and ultimately of a larger African world" (p.3).

CHAPTER 3

Coming to America

African presence in America did not begin with slavery. Africans were among the early explorers who came to America. Banks (1997) records that an African was with Christopher Columbus during his last voyage to America in 1502, and Africans were among the first non-Native American settlers, and they, in fact, helped to establish St. Augustine, Florida, in 1565.

Genesis

African presence in America as slaves began in the early 1600, when twenty blacks were brought to Jamestown to work in the Virginia plantations (Gutek, 1986). Later, millions and millions were unwillingly packed into slave ships and transported to the New World to meet the growing need for plantation labor.

Although the original Africans to the Americas came here unwillingly, the new wave of African immigrants to America came here on their own to seek a better life for themselves and their families. Since they were voluntary immigrants, they were able to stay together with their kinfolks and were able to maintain their language and cultural values. They have found ways to preserve their cultural heritage and identity, which was denied those who came unwillingly, and who were deliberately separated from their families.

The recent African immigrants were driven by the same force, which drove other immigrant groups to come to America. Most of these immigrant groups came for political, economic, and/or religious reasons.

41

Most Europeans, for example, came to America for economic reasons. Majority of them were peasants who were deprived or feared the loss of their lands (Banks, 1997).

The Irish left their beloved homeland to escape the poverty, and tyranny created by English colonial policies. They left to escape from oppression and economic hardship.

The Chinese came to America to seek survival from harsh economic conditions. They came to seek sanctuary from the intense conflicts in China caused by the British Opium Wars, and to escape the turmoil of peasant rebellions.

The Japanese came to ease the burden of taxation and to escape economic hardships. They came to seek a better life for themselves and their families.

The Jews came to flee from pogroms and religious persecution in Russia (Takaki, 1993). They came in search of the Promised Land.

The Hispanics came to America to escape the economic depression in their native countries (Friedman, 1998). They came to look for better jobs and opportunities.

Equally, the Africans came to seek a better life and to escape the disastrous political, economic, and social conditions of their countries. They came to escape from pogroms and religious persecutions. They came in search of freedom and dignity.

Exodus

These African immigrants to the United States are highly educated, urbanized and have one of the highest per capita incomes of any immigrant group (Speer, 1994).

As we have seen, like all other immigrant groups, the Africans came to seek refuge from political upheaval, severely depressed economy, ravaging civil wars, excessive poverty, and unequal distribution of wealth. Their pattern and timing of immigration also corresponded with economic depression and political turmoil of the continent. The desire to migrate was fueled, intensified, and made more dramatic by civil war, turmoil, violence, poor economic and social conditions, and violation of human rights, unfortunate characteristics that had exposed the continent's weak democratic base.

In Nigeria, for example, many young people left the country to seek better opportunities in America, inspired by the stories of "freedom, liberty, and opportunity." The wave of migration intensified after the civil war of 1966, a war that sipped through the pores of a healthy nation and ravaged it beyond repair. They left by the hundreds and by the thousands.

Thousands spend endless days and nights at the American embassy hoping to be granted visas to travel to America. Many were lured by the dream of crossing the "Red Sea" to the Promised Land, a land across many oceans and seas, a land flowing with milk and honey, a land with boundless opportunities for employment and success. Most of them came initially as sojourners, who came to get higher education, make a lot of money in America, and return to their homelands. Majority of them are still in America.

Numbers

Pulled by the political instability and economic hardships in their homelands and pulled by the American dream and seized by curiosity, these Africans crossed the seas and oceans, leaving behind their fathers and mothers, wives and children, businesses and jobs. Today, both young and old in Africa want to come to America to experience this great land of milk and honey, the land where darkness never falls.

America has become the stuff of boundless dreams for African men and women, young and old. In growing numbers, they come with extravagant hopes and lavish dreams.

Millions line the American embassy everyday to seek immigrant visas to the United States, and in great numbers, they are turned down. Even professionals abandoned their jobs to migrate: lawyers, doctors, nurses, college professors, and

43

the list goes on and on. They would sell their belongings and give up their "birth rights" just to come to America. An African immigrant in Washington, D. C. recalled how he hesitated becoming an American citizen for two decades, but later decided to do so; thus forfeiting rights to his father's inheritance in Ethiopia (N'Diaye, 1997).

Although many have come, most have experienced disappointment, and have expressed the desire to return. Because most of them had sold all their belongings and given up their trade, returning home would be more devastating. They, therefore, had no other recourse but to stay and "dig the ditch."

Most practicing doctors in their countries now find themselves working as "Sitters" and "Psychiatric Technicians" in the hospitals because they could not practice medicine without obtaining the American medical license. Established lawyers in their home countries find themselves delivering pizza because they do not have the license to practice law in America. Many of them have become newspaper boys, distributing daily news from door to door in the wee hours of the morning. Some have ended up hanging themselves. Some have died of strokes and heart attacks, and others have kept the faith.

An immigrant told a story of his cousin, a Barrister, who won the immigrant lottery, abandoned his successful practice, and came to America "to make it big." He left his wife and four children at home with the hope of getting things in order in America before they would join him. Well, when he came, he squatted with his cousin for about six months, trying to secure employment with a law firm, or perhaps open his own law firm.

When none of these ideas seemed to materialize and funds were running low, he was compelled to find something to do to hold on. His first job was at McDonalds, where he was hired to wash dishes and clean the floors and the parking lot. His brother came home from his job two days later and found his body dangling from the ceiling fan. He left his wife and children at home with little or no hope of surviving. His body was flown home and buried.

Migrating to America has not been easy for the Africans. Their solidarity has suffered strains as their culture comes in contact with a way of life not developed to accommodate them and due to the inevitable ethnic differences arising from rapid political and economic growth of which they have no place. They face the problem of racism and alienation as they struggle to be admitted, even by their own people, the African-Americans. Some of them complain that the African immigrants were taking all their jobs.

Most of them have continued to work menial jobs with minimum wages. Most are unemployed and poor, living under bridges and homeless shelters. Furthermore, as a people, they face the oppressive and discriminatory practices of their Anglo and even African-American hosts. That, added to the stereotypical view of the Africans by the Americans, has created further problems of social and political integration.

Most Africans initially came as sojourners who came to get higher education, make a lot of money in America, and return to their homelands to take up higher positions in their countries' marketplace. When they arrived, contrary to their expectations, the "real jobs" were not real open for them.

Almost every one of them experienced the hardship of a "chicken in a foreign land," standing on one leg. They found themselves laborers in the low-wage jobs, washing dishes in fast food restaurants, delivering pizza, cleaning linens at hotels, changing diapers in nursing homes, picking trash off the highways, and driving taxi cabs.

They did it all without complaining, because they had an ultimate goal: to survive and get education. So they worked endless hours and shifts and still found time to go to school and maintain their minimum immigration course load requirements.

Most of them have done well for themselves, and most of them have contributed immensely to the economy of the American society. They are making their marks in America in different areas of life, in business ventures and entrepreneurship, in education, churches, and communal associations.

In the field of sports, for example, Hakeem "The Dream" Olajuwom, the NBA All-Star with the Houston Rockets, Dikembe Mutombo, the NBA Four-time Defensive Player of the Year, Manut Bol, and a host of others, have brought African immigrant group to the spotlight. African immigrants are represented in politics, in business, in medicine, in law, and in the field of education.

There are many African educators in America today. There are teachers in American classrooms and professors in universities around the nation. African immigrants have produced doctors and nurses who save lives in American hospitals and lawyers who litigate cases in American courtrooms.

The going has not been easy. The unfortunate situation, however, is that some of those who have "made it" or even those who are still striving to make it will go back home to visit, but would not tell the true story of survival in America. Even when they would do, no one would believe them.

Everyone wants to come to America and "suffer" just like every one else. The general sentiment was "Since you made it, I will make it too." Some would think that those stories of struggle and hardship were meant to discourage them from going to America and becoming like them—educated and successful.

Africans are still struggling to participate fully in the social processes that lead to effective integration into the mainstream American society. They however, have continued to work hard to keep their tie with one another in an attempt to continue to maintain a responsible, visible hold on the society. Everyone has a role to play.

"The Arrow of God"

Most African countries today are beginning to experience dramatic changes in governance. Although there are still some internal strives to be settled here and there, peace, stability, and democracy have begun to exert their presence in the lives of the people and in the continent as a whole.

In some of these countries where human suffering have been perpetuated by dictatorships and autocratic rule, it has taken Divine intervention to rid the countries and their citizens of the agony of helplessness. The arrow of God struck, piercing the chests of hatred, crime, embezzlement, and selfishness and clearing the grounds for better leadership and democracy.

Why they left - negative view

"This is Our Chance"

In Nigeria, for example, the sudden and mysterious death of President Sani Abacha awakened the nation to its responsibility and ushered in a new era. New doors opened for the Nigerian immigrants in the United States who felt that this was their chance to make a difference, a chance to return and take part in the governance of their country and states. Most of them went home to run for political positions in their home states, and most are now serving in different areas of government.

African immigrants fled from pogroms and economic disaster. They fled from poor living conditions due to political greed. They ran away from poverty and poor health conditions due to lack of adequate health care. They ran away from hostility, conflicts, bribery, and corruption. Now they feel the need to make life better for those they left behind. They feel strongly that this is their chance to utilize their resources to make a difference in their home countries.

Recently the shift has been toward working to rebuild their countries, and they have done so by embarking on numerous projects in their home countries, villages, and towns. Most cultural celebrations and festivals now have fund-raising component built in. Their goal, aspiration, and mission are well articulated and expressed in the speeches of the various organization presidents. In his welcome address, the president of the Old Bende Cultural Association said:

> *Many times the sons and daughters of Bende have sat here by the rivers of Babylon; and we have many times wept when we remembered our Zion. But we just don't sit here and weep. We have*

47

provided scholarships over the years to Bende students at home. We have embarked on a book drive to expand our home university library, and we have continued to reach out to our beloved ones at home in many special ways. We have called you tonight to lend a helping hand as we commit to supporting the education of our children at home. Your generous donations will be appreciated.

In his welcome speech at one of the festivals in 1997, the president of Ika Progressive Organization also said:

We all do know that one of the greatest sufferings facing our people at home is lack of clean water supply. Our organization has decided to improve the situation and make sure that adequate clean water reaches our underprivileged people. Our goal is to raise $100,000.00 over a period of time, and we cannot achieve this without honest generosity.

Speaking during one of their festivals held in Houston, the spokesperson for the Ga Adangme Kpee of Greater Houston said:

Festivals in Ghana and indeed Africa bring families together. Tonight, we are grateful that family members have traveled from far and near to be part of this celebration. As we observe the festival this year, I'm confident and convinced that we will be proudly leaving a legacy to our children. This was the same legacy that our forefathers left us. Let us therefore strive to instill in our children the best values. It is a moral obligation to which all of us are morally bound to uphold.... To this end, we must not forget the plight of our fathers and mothers, our brothers and sisters, and of course our children back at home. Let us strive to connect with them as often as we can....

A Cock on a Foreign Soil

Having come from a different world, Africa immigrants expressed different types of shocks, ranging from direct discriminatory practices to indiscriminate acts of stereotyping. Although some have worked their way out of such shocks, others, especially the new arrivals, are still standing on one leg, like a cock on a foreign soil, hoping that someday, they would put both legs down.

Although some have overcome their shock, most continue to experience it on a daily basis in their interaction with the dominant culture.

Most shock occur when they find themselves exposed to new concepts to which they have no knowledge of, and which is contrary to their own way of life. Some came with degrees from their home countries to find out that those degrees needed added certification to be good. For some of them, their degrees and transcripts were sent to be evaluated, only to return with a lower evaluation rating or high deficiency.

Many of them have experienced discrimination in one form or another in employment and education. One immigrant talked about his experience as a student:

> There was nothing I wrote in my English Composition class that merited a 'C.' Every paper I turned in had red marks all over it. The instructor saw me as a 'D" student when I first introduced myself. He even asked me to drop the class and enroll in a remedial class. I was an English major back home. That frustrated me a whole lot, and forced me to change my major.

Most African immigrants today have achieved stable employment in skilled occupations. Most live in suburbs and make decent living, but they live in separate areas of town as opposed to creating a neighborhood or community of their own. One immigrant added humor to his comment:

> You can never find Africans living together like Asians and Hispanics and the rest of them. We all want to live in big houses and drive big cars, but have no money to buy gas.

However, the significant factor that lowers the average African's economic status is not the big cars and huge houses, but family size. No matter what his means of livelihood is, the African immigrant is aware that he or she has it in his

49

or her power to do more than provide for himself and his immediate family, but must and will provide for his extended family.

The extended family

Africans have very large families and extended families; hence, the ratio of dependence on the income of an average African in America is considerably larger than their African-American brothers. An average African living in America probably has parents, grandparents, siblings, uncles, aunts, and other relatives at home that depend solely on him, and these are in addition to his immediate family here in America---his wife and children.

Western Union and Money Gram have identified themselves with the African immigrant groups, knowing that they represent a significant part of their business clientele. Almost all African immigrants in America send money home to parents and relatives. There are others of them who, due to the pressure of acculturation and financial constraint, have deviated from this strong cultural norm. Some even offer scholarships to deserving African immigrant children.

"The Lost Finger"

Due to the overwhelming influence of American culture on immigrant Africans, most of them find themselves conforming to Anglo cultural patterns. Most Africans gradually find themselves making transition from their traditional values and behaviors to American or Western values and modes of behavior. The factors that have influenced such transition include the number of years they have resided in America, their desire to become "Americanized" based on the notion that the American way is the ideal way.

The "Americanization" of African immigrants is minimal. For the most part, they have proven to be "indigestible" and therefore have great difficulty melting in the same pot like all other groups. No matter how much they try, they have always been identified as Africans, in appearance, in language, in accent, and in different other ways.

Feminism

There are growing concerns about the effect of Western feminism on African women. Most African women are solely committed to household duties and taking care of their children and husbands, but the process of acculturation has caused them to become liberated from traditional constraints, and majority of them venture into the workforce.

African immigrant parents also worry about the effect of acculturation on their children. They worry about their children losing respect for the elderly and their daughter, especially, asserting the American prerogative of choosing a career path and a spouse on their own.

It is important to note that not all Africans want to give it all up. Most still maintain their ethnic loyalty and cultural identity; hence, a wide range of differences exist in the extent to which they are acculturated to Anglo society.

Many Africans have changed their native names and have adopted American names. Those who did not completely change their names have "modified" their names to suit the dominant culture. Unfortunately, when these names are changed or modified, they lose their original meanings and identity.

Despite these pressures to belong and become an integral part of the mainstream, one center still holds: strong culture traditions of the Africans, their language, and strong family ties have, to a large extent, limited their assimilation.

However, Africans have made and have continued to make valuable contributions to American culture. They rejoice in the successful transportation of a cultural heritage whose diversity and dynamism enriches American life in all aspects.

African arts and crafts thrive in America as Americans and the world have come to value the indigenous African arts, crafts, and culture. Their art beautify the walls of most homes, offices, and business places in America.

Most Americans today wear braids, clothing, earrings, and anklets that are of African origin. There are many today who pierce their noses and ears and other body parts for beautification purposes.

African foods are gradually making their way into American culture, as many loyal Africans have continued to eat those foods by which they were

biculturalism

nurtured and bread. Als[...]e becoming a part of American musical scene.

The Best of Both World

Africans, like members of other ethnic groups, are part of two cultures, a process known as biculturalism. They can comfortably switch between mainstreaming culture and African culture. While in a professional setting, at work or in the midst of colleagues, they tend to "do as the Romans do." At home or in their community settings, they are Africans, in dress, in the type of food they choose to eat, the music they like to listen to, and so on.

One immigrant described how he would go to work and feast on enchiladas and other Mexican foods, but would come home and "pounce" on his *fufu* with *egusi* or *amala with ewedu, and so on*. He also discussed how his wife would expect him to act American in some cases and not in others to her benefit. They seem to enjoy the best of both worlds, being African women in one sense and American women in the other.

The Pendulum Effect

There is nothing wrong with being bicultural; it is an inevitable aspect of being a minority in a dominant culture. There are some Africans who wish to retain their rich cultural heritage and legacy and want to be identified with their roots. However, there are those among them who try to become completely assimilated into the mainstream culture, but find that they end up not belonging to any.

The new culture did not completely accept them, and the old culture did not completely leave them. They find themselves dangling between two worlds, a phenomenon that I refer to as *the pendulum effect.*

52

CHAPTER 4

One People, One Destiny

African organizations abound in America, ranging from A to Z (Algeria to Zimbabwe). In Houston, for example, there is the African Community Organization, whose goal is to unite all Africans and also provide protection to its people and meet the general need of the community. In addition to this umbrella organization, other organizations exist, ranging from country folks to even clan and family associations who, in case of death, arrange to take home the bodies of the deceased.

These organizations hold annual conventions all across the United States. They converge in Denver, New York, Dallas, Houston, Baltimore, Atlanta, Los Angeles, New Orleans, Oklahoma, and so on. They find time to reenact the rituals that take place in their homelands and to pass them on to their American-born children. They come, as one of them said, to sensitize themselves to the needs of their children, their people in America and those at home.

"Bele m a Ipaye"

When the Rivers State Foundation, USA converged in Dallas, Texas, in 1999, during their 9th Annual Convention, its president, in his welcome address, called on all members of the organization and Africans to come together to revive the social, political, and economical strength of their people. During the ceremonies, the audience experienced a taste and enchantment of Africa. Authentic African foods of different kinds were served; cultural dances were performed, including performances by the *Bele m a Ipaye* and the masquerade.

"Pearls of the Nile River"

The African Cultural Exchange presents Africa Day annually to the thrill of everyone. This event brings together all Africans and friends to celebrate Africa. During the festivals, the *Pearls of Nile Valley* Cultural Group treated the audience with spectacular performances. The dancers body movements and rhythmic gestures accentuate the elegance and body control that is Africa.

The African Cultural Exchange also involves itself in different activities. It is involved in the creation, implementation, and operation of educational enrichment programs that benefit, not only Africans and African children, but all children and adults from other cultures who are interested in learning about Africa. Its dance group, *The Pearls of Nile Valley*, made up of men and women from Kenya, Tanzania, and Uganda, takes the audience on a tour of Africa through drumming, song, dance, story-telling and more.

"Egbe Omo Yoruba"

When the *Egbe Omo Yoruba*, a National Association of Yoruba Descendants in North America, convened in Irving, Texas in 1997, it brought Africa to Irving through cultural displays and authentic African foods and music. This organization has chapters across the United States, and they all came to strengthen their ties and to work together to rebuild their homeland.

These chapters include the *Egbe Isokan Yoruba* in Washington, DC, *the Egbe Omo Oduduwa* in New York City, *the Oduduwa Unity Club* in Greensboro, North Carolina, the *Yoruba International Union* in Dallas, Texas, the *Yoruba Omo Oduduwa* in Houston, Texas, *the Yoruba peoples Congress* in Chicago, *the Isokan Yoruba* of Georgia, *the Yoruba Community* of Ohio. There are also *the Yoruba Cultural and Development Organization* in Philadelphia, *the Oduduwa Heritage Organization* in Oakland, California, *the Egbe Omo Yoruba* in Staten Island, New York, *the Egbe Omo Yoruba* in Kansas, *the Kiriji Movement* in San Francisco, *and the Yoruba League* in Los Angeles, California.

In his welcome address, the National President of the association eloquently sang the praises of their ancestors. He spoke of the foundation work of Oduduwa, the patriotism of Imoremi Aja Soro, the institutional building achievement of Oranmiyan, the sacrifice of Owa Obokun, and the valor of Ogedengbe, Sodeke, and Ogumola. He also paid homage to their most recent departed fathers, such as Awolowo, Akintola, Abiola, and Ajasin.

"Our Sentiment"

He also called on all Yoruba sons and daughters to keep the fire of culture, language, education, and economic prosperity burning for the sake of the future generation, to unite in providing effective healthcare facilities for their people, and to take care of the families of those who have been unjustly incarcerated.

Several other African organizations echo similar sentiment. During the gathering of the Enugu State Women Group in 1999 in Houston, Texas, the president of the organization reiterated one of the goals of the women of this organization. She emphasized the need to teach their younger generations to love, respect, and care for one another in order for them to have a foundation necessary to survive in this world.

Also, in his address during the organization's convention in 1997, a representative of the Ika Progressive Organization said:

> *Our main objective of incepting this reputable organization twelve years ago is to promote our traditional heritage, foster a common goal, and instill in our children our love and traditional values.*

The spokesperson of the Igbo Peoples' Congress, in his 1993 remarks during the Igbo Day celebration said:

> *As we celebrate this day, do not forget that our uniqueness lies in the diversity of our cultural heritage. Let us therefore stop and*

recognize that only our collaborative efforts and dedications will bring back to our families those cultural values and practices we are now on the verge of losing.

In 1996, a spokesperson of the Aniocha-Ashimili Association said in his speech to the people at their annual gathering that one of the challenges facing them as parents was to induct their growing children into the traditions of their parents.

The African immigrants celebrate festivals, perform cultural dances, prepare and eat ethnic foods, and recreate scenes from their homeland. These festivals attract the attention of those in the high places. During the Ugandan North American Association 10th Anniversary Convention in 1998, for instance, the president of the United States, Bill Clinton, wrote a letter wishing them a wonderful event and expressing the profound and lasting contributions people from every region of the world have made to American society.

Also, the then Governor of Texas, George W. Bush, sent his greetings to the organization. In the letter, he commended the Ugandan-Americans for enhancing the traditions that are part of American history---entrepreneurship, a sense of community where neighbor helps neighbor, and love for family.

During these ceremonies, the kids were given the opportunity to perform cultural dances. Included in these performances were the Kuumba Kids and the Hounaa Kids. The young drummers and dancers mesmerized the crowd with an exciting rhythmic beating of the drums, the graceful movement of their bodies, and the fascinating methodic motion of their footwork.

It is in rituals, dance and music that the indigenous African artistic expression reaches its heights, each community having its own ritual dances and musical forms to celebrate major occasions as they are celebrated in their homelands.

African talent and creative expression are exhibited on the skill of the drummers weaving their intricate and ancient patterns of rhythm and the dancers flexibility as they move their bodies and maintain their footwork with precision, stomping and stamping.

The Homowo Festival

The Ghana community in United States also held its annual seasonal festival in Houston, Texas. This festival, the *Homowo*, brought together members of the Ga community to sensitize themselves about their cultural values and to solicit protection, help, and guidance from their ancestors.

The aims of the Ga Adangme Kpee are to unite members in the bonds of friendship, good fellowship, and mutual understanding, to provide a forum for the full and free discussion of all matters of interest to the Ga Adangme community, to promote social, cultural, educational, and recreational activities for its members, to promote greater knowledge and understanding of the Ga Adangme people and their culture. The goal of the organization also includes assisting the needy through donations and many other means that may be at the association's disposal.

According to an insider, the *Homowo* is patterned after the Jewish Passover, in that unleavened cornmeal is used for the *Homowo* ritual meal. The festival began with the *Homowo* prayer:

> *On this solemn Saturday of our ancestors, we thank Thee O God*
> *that we are able to celebrate this year's Homowo Festival. May*
> *we enjoy the fruits of GBO and the products of GBO-E-NAA.*
> *TWA! TWA! TWA! MONANYE ABA: YAO!*

On this very occasion, after the preparation of the meal which was done on Saturday at dawn, merrymaking ensued to welcome all the Ga Endgames who had come from far and near to be a part of this festival. Later on in the evening, the celebration began. It was time to consume the ritual meal and the palm-soup. First, the *Wulomo* (Chief Priest) went around and sprinkled some of the *Kpoikpoi* (ritual meal) at different points for the departed fathers to partake also. Then he began to say a solemn Homowo prayer, pouring libation as he spoke.

Although important aspects of the ritual were omitted due to the laws of America, the Wulomo assured all the Ga Endgames that their ancestors understood their plight. They knew that they were in a foreign country and are very proud of them for their effort to reenact this ritual. Then he said, "We will continue to follow our tradition and pass on the torch to our children and the children yet unborn   "Twa Twa! Omannye aba! Yao!"

Nostalgia

The Akwa   African culture to live in Houston at Adam   State convention when they showcased their a_____   dances from all parts of the state. The Ibibio masquerade, known historically for its fierce and awe-inspiring appearance, created intense nostalgia.

Singing, dancing, clapping, and beating of drums are essential to many ceremonies of the African immigrants. During these ceremonies, children of African immigrants also perform. For example, the Old Bende group of the Igbo has a children's dance troupe choreographed by Darlington Ndubuike. They are taught the traditional dance steps that imitate the dance steps of the native dancers.

Through carefully chosen lyrics and dance movements, the choreographer recreates a world reminiscent to that found in their native land. Through the dancing, singing, and body movement, the children learn about their cultural values.

There are three groups of dancers among the Old Bende cultural group---the men, the women, and the children. Each of these groups dances to a different tune with different rhythmic patterns.

The men represent the warriors who have returned successfully from war with a neighboring tribe and are exhibiting their "trophy" and prowess. The dance involves a vigorous shaking of the upper body with an intricate, methodic footwork and hand gestures. Balance is a key aspect of this dance presentation. The lead dancer is required to balance his warlike headdress on his head while dancing.

This particular dance is the type that brings together all the gods, the ancestors, and all the heavenly crew to celebrate with humankind. Every male is invited to participate in this dance. In putting the dance steps together, the choreographer emphasizes precision in dynamism.

One of the dancers expressed a deep concern about the loss of some of the main features of the dance:

> *Back home, this dance is done with palm wine in a large clay pot. The dancers hold live cocks in their hands as they perform. Our hands are tied here. We cannot dance with a life rooster because of the culture we are in. I'm very happy that we are able to do the much we are doing to show our children what our culture is like. I hope they take it from us and run with it.*

The women's dance is a sophisticated assemblage of rhythm, movement, and song. The lyrics teach as well as intoxicate both the dancers and the audience. Almost all the time, the audience joins the women on the dance floor as participant observers.

The children's dance incorporates some of the dance steps of the men and some of the women. The children range from age 5 to 17. They are taught cooperative work, the essence of uniformity in diversity, and the importance of accurate timing. Because of their age, their dance steps are more intricately choreographed, allowing them the full use of their flexibility, elasticity, and youthful exuberance without sacrificing grace and appeal.

The activities of the group range from monthly cultural gatherings to yearly cultural exhibitions. The yearly South African cookout celebrated in the summer in the Washington area brings communities together seasonally (Cook and Belanus, 1997). During this event, the women would congregate in the kitchen, singing, sharing cooking ideas, and making specialty dishes for the celebration. The men would hang out together in the backyard with the barbecue grill, preparing the *imbuzi ne mvy* (goat and lamb) meat they had slaughtered earlier for meat (Cook and Belanus, 1997).

In the greater Washington metropolitan area, organizations and groups like the Nwannedinamba Social Club of Nigeria, the Asante Kotoko Association, and the Ethiopian Business Association contribute immensely in the revitalization of the traditional norms, values, and civic unity among the Africans (Olumba, 1995). These activities revitalize them and sensitize them. They also provide the needed process of enculturation.

The Mbaise group in the Houston area also celebrated its New Yam festival, and it was one of the most thrilling and cultural learning experiences of its kind. This celebration was scheduled for 9:00 p.m. The hall was ready, decorated with traditional African hats on the walls, palm trees and artifacts.

Tables were covered with yellow, red and silver garments. Just in front of the high table was a shrine---piles of firewood, two carved wooden figures sitting on both sides of the piled wood and another carved figure standing in the rear, a wooden chair covered with leopard skin, and a palm-tree standing in a pot. Beside the chair lay two elephant tusks, a ceramic jar and an old wooden walking stick. Tables were set in a rectangular pattern, leaving the center of the hall virtually empty except for the yam tubers that were placed in front of the shrine.

At about 11:00 p.m., the Master of Ceremonies (MC) was introduced. He apologized for the delay in the start of the event and promised everybody a good time.

Someone sitting across the hall commented, "He is talking as if lateness is something new. Don't we always start everything late?" Everyone laughed at the joke.

The MC reminded everyone that it was African time, and that people needed to reset their watches to match his time. Then he began his monologue:

60

The farmers have come home. The harvest is plentiful. We are here, therefore, to celebrate this bountiful harvest and to give thanks to the gods for guiding and protecting us all through the farming season.

He paused for few seconds as if to allow a murmur of approval to sweep the crowd.

Before we do anything today, we must follow the tradition. Therefore, I will call on the person who will coordinate tonight's rituals.

He called on someone he described as "A man of timber and caliber." The people applauded. A man of an average height stood up from among the rest of the people.

He was gorgeously dressed and adorned in his native regalia---a long gray robe over a red wraparound called "*George*", a round red cap made of velvet material and decorated with shiny buttons all around it. A yellow feather perched on the side of the cap. A row of beads hung from his neck. He was holding a walking stick and a fan. He took his wife in his left hand and proceeded toward the table.

His wife was wearing the women's type *George* material wrapped around her waist---one longer than the other. Her hair was long and hung loosely on her shoulders. Her blouse was of satin lace material. The people continued to applaud. The Ritual lord, as they addressed him, waved at the people with his fan as he walked to the table. He acknowledged the shrine with a wave of his fan.

The MC called on other elders who would support the Ritual lord. As he called their names, they got up, took their wives and walked to the "high table". Each elder is also geared traditionally. Most of them were holding fans made of cowhide and leather, and each fan had the elder's name or/and title inscribed on it. Some were holding whisks, some walking sticks.

As each elder got to the table, he greeted the Ritual lord and the elder that was there before him. The form of greeting was also in the traditional manner. When everyone was settled in his seat and applaud subsided, the MC gave the microphone to one of the elders who stood to speak.

The entire place was quiet. Despite the huge crowd, one could hear a pin drop at this moment. The elder cleared his throat and began:

We are here to celebrate the "Ahiajioku festival. This is a time when the landowner and the laborer come to one table to celebrate fecundity, to thank the gods and Mother Earth. Yam is not the only crop that we eat. What we are doing here is an annual traditional event to give thanks to the Almighty. As we celebrate, we also hope that the next harvest will be bigger. Amen.

Before we proceed, I would like for us to present the kolanut. Kolanut is unlike every other nut. It is an instrument of welcome. It is a significant aspect of our culture. If you are offered kolanut as a visitor, it means that you are quite welcome. If you accept it and eat, it means that you have come as a friend, not a foe. No libation is complete without kolanut.

He scanned the hall in silence. Everybody was quiet and watching. He walked to the shrine in front of the high table, stood there for few minutes in silence, turned facing the audience. Then he turned to the elders, cleared his throat and began:

With respect to all the elders here and the chiefs. With respect to all the people present. I would have preferred to do this in our native dialect, but for the fact that we have guests who may not understand me.

He cleared his throat again and paused for a few moments. During this time, silence swept the entire hall. He continued:

I would like all representatives from every neighboring tribe to come and take a piece of the kolanut.

When all the neighboring tribes have taken, he called on the different countries of Africa, then the Caribbean, Mexico, China, and America. Then he asked all those who took kolanut on behalf of their people to stand up. They all stood up, and he offered a short prayer, blessing the kolanut.

He called all the elders to join him at this time. They all walked up to where he was standing---in front of the shrine. Each elder took a piece of kolanut from the tray and took a position by the shrine until they formed a semi-circle. The audience watched with a crest of enthusiasm.

He began to perform the ritual. Each time he called on the ancestors, he threw a piece of the kolanut on the carved figures and all over the shrine.

As the elders were responding, the audience joined. The hall exploded in a big round of applause of excitement. They appeared to have been reassured as the Chief Ritualist and the elders walked back to their seats. Some young men broke the remaining kolanuts and passed them around to everybody. Meanwhile, the DJ played some traditional music. There was loud talking and chatting. People were stretching their vocal cords in an attempt to converse with people sitting close to them. It did not even appear as if they were screaming because of the loud noise in the hall.

Meanwhile, they began to place bottles of drinks on the high table and on all the other tables as well. They were bottles of champagne. Almost immediately, champagne corks began to fly up and across the hall. Everywhere in the hall, one could here the sound of a popping champagne bottle. One could also feel the excitement. People's faces shone with blessedness and peace.

The Chief Ritualist stood, cleared his throat, and began again to speak:

We have our elders here. We also have the chiefs.
I am inviting all the titled chiefs and elders to accompany me once
again to the shrine. We also invite all the members representing
each clan and tribe to accompany us as well. This is one of the
most important aspects of our ceremony tonight.

He did not call the representatives of the other nations to accompany them at this time perhaps due to the nature of the ritual to be performed. This aspect of the ritual was for those who understood the culture or was meant for the elders of the tribe who were familiar with the world of the ancestors.

Meanwhile, all those called walked to the shrine, holding their cups of wine in their hands. The Chief Ritualist picked up one piece of yam tuber and showed it to the elders. They nodded their heads in agreement. He began to speak:

> *Ladies and gentlemen, this is the time that we thank the gods for giving us riches. This is the time we remember all the hardships we went through during planting season. We thank God Almighty for the fruitful harvest. We remember also all those who have gone before us and who are interceding and making the way for us. This is an emotional time. Please bear with me.*

He walked quietly and silently closer to the shrine, stirred at it for few seconds and raised his cup above his head. Every elder did the same.
He poured the drinks in his cup on the shrine. The elders did the same. They knocked their cups together as in a toast, and then drank what was left.

As the Chief Ritualist and the elders cheered, everyone else followed. What one could hear at this time was the cranking of cups as they knocked on each other and the noise from the people cheering. In the background, a traditional music played. Everyone began to drink.

In his opening speech, the leader of the organization began:

> *I welcome everyone personally. Today, we are celebrating a bountiful harvest. We are proud to present tonight, and are honored to have each one of you in our midst as we celebrate the New Yam.*
> *It is no coincidence that in almost every culture worldwide, different socio-economic and ethnic groups have often set aside*

special times for events celebrating and thanking God for that year's harvest of plenty. The celebration of bountiful harvest therefore transcends almost every culture and remains an age-long tradition that has been passed on from one generation to the other, irrespective of societal advances.

Regardless of how advanced or how primitive or how diversified or how homogenous many societal groups are, a common denominator, that is, that of a celebration of a bountiful harvest, links each group across the board. "Iri-ji" or a celebration of new yam harvest is an important aspect of Igbo culture. It is an annual event, which brings the Igbo together wherever they are.

In Igboland, the festival is observed in the month of August. The ceremony embraces a lot of activities involving dancing, masquerades and feasting.

The day of the "Iri-ji" starts with the women cleaning up the major roadways and the market square. At about noon, all the villages assemble at the market square to commence the ceremony.

People look forward to this day because it is mostly during this time that young people from far and wide come home to woo their would-be husbands and wives. The day's activities usually end with exchange of visits.

In modern times, as it is today, the theme, though significantly symbolizing a celebration of harvest, takes on new definitions, such as that of life, good luck, better goal achievement, greater fulfillment, or an overall betterment in each individual's life. The Igbo here in Houston, therefore, join together in welcoming you, their friends and well- wishers alike in this celebration of harvest, and wish you all the great things that they wish themselves and their families.

Our celebration tonight is so symbolic, yet so cultural and rich in origin and reflects upon thanking a higher power for watching over us all and providing for us rich, plentiful and abundant harvest within the past year and hoping for the same in the upcoming year. Thank you and welcome.

There were some Americans in the audience who were dressed in the Igbo traditional attire, both Whites and Blacks. There were Latinos also, but they were not "traditionally" dressed. Meanwhile, a group of women set a table in front of the high table, beside the shrine, and placed pots of food on it---boiled yams, soup, roasted hen.

Six women, identically attired, stood behind the food table ready to serve.

The Chief Ritualist walked to the food table and picked up a piece of yam. He turned to the high table and beckoned on the elders. They rose and walked to him. He led the way to the shrine. They surrounded the shrine in a half-circle. Everyone watched in stunned silence.

Again, he began to call on the ancestors and the gods of the land. As he spoke, at the end of each line, he threw pieces of yam on the shrine. The elders and the audience watched in complete silence. He reached to the table and picked up a bowl of soup and poured some of the soup on the shrine. He also took a piece of hen and threw it on the shrine. He clapped his hands as if to make sure that none of the pieces meant for the ancestors and the gods stuck in his hand. He turned around, thrusting his hand in the air bellowed:

	Igbo, kwenu!
Audience:	*Yaah!*
	Igbo, kwenu!
Audience:	*Yaah!*
	Igbo, kwezuenu!
Audience:	*Yaah!*

Then he concluded:

We can now eat the new yam. Please be sure there's enough to go around. Our visitors are invited to taste this traditional symbol. Thank you very much.

Everyone applauded. The elders greeted him in the traditional manner. They all walked back to their seats. A loud chatting noise swept the crowd momentarily.

The audience applauded again as he took his seat. Music began to play in the background. The women began to serve the food. Some others came and offered helping hands, carrying plates of food to the tables. The feast had begun. It was about 3:15 a.m. in the morning.

After all the eating and drinking, the
Women-folks performed a cultural drama, depicting the process of farming in Igboland---from planting to harvest. This was immediately followed by a traditional dance performance by the men, called "Abigbo."

Right after the men's dance, the women came on with their "*Agbachaa E Kuru Nwa*" dance. Celebration was in full swing. It was in the wee hours of the morning, but no one seemed to border.

After the women's dance, it was time for the masquerade to emanate from the under world. Masquerade epitomizes the Igbo artistic ensemble---the mask, the costumes, the drums, and the people. It is the manifestation of the unity between them and their ancestors.

Soon, a young man came in with a bell. He was dressed in multi-colored striped skirt, yellow A-shirt, red cap, with feather hanging on it, and rattles on his ankles. He rang the bell three times. All eyes focused on him. He went toward the high table and rang the bell again. The elders nodded. He rang the bell again and again. Then he began to jump and hop on one leg in a circle. The audience watched in stunned silence. He hopped and jumped for a while and left. Then the audience cheered.

Everyone continued to look towards the direction from which he had come in and through which he left. Soon, the drummers came in, dressed just like the "Bellman". They sat down on a bench set for them. There were six drummers in all and one other person holding a rattling staff.

The drums beat and beat and beat, rising and falling in a head-swelling crescendo. Suddenly, the music stopped. Somewhere outside, a sound was heard. It was like a bullroarer. First it was distant. Then it came closer and closer. All the elders and the Chief Ritualist stood and came out to the open floor.

The drummers began again. This time, the tempo was higher. The floor throbbed. The crowd stood on their feet, gazing at one direction. Soon, from behind the shrine, a huge masquerade appeared. It was wearing a dark mask with three horns and huge, bulging red and white eyeballs. Its red tongue stuck out like one in a frantic seizure.

The costume the masquerade wore was made of multi-colored dyed raffia. A huge bell hung behind him. The rattles on his ankles and waist shook in agitated frenzy. He dashed into the hall, stumping and stamping. The Chief Ritualist sipped some drink from the cup and blew it on the mask.

The man holding the rattle reached into the leather bag hanging on his left shoulder, brought out something and threw it on the mask. It was a raw egg. It smashed on the forehead of the mask and splattered all over. Meanwhile, the masquerade stood still with his arms folded across his chest.

Someone emerged from the other side of the hall blowing on a flute. It was a wooden flute. The masquerade turned around, waved his whip in the air and took off running. Stampede overtook the crowd in that direction. Meanwhile, the drums continued to beat. The faces of the drummers glittered with perspiration.

The masquerade came back to the center of the hall and began to dance to the intricate rhythm of the lead drum. He danced and danced and danced. People threw money from wherever they were standing. Some of the money fell short to the floor. Some tried to touched the masquerade. It was a spectacular sight.

The masquerade stumped, whirled around several times and took off. It was gone. The crowd applauded and roared. The drummers played for few more minutes and packed up. It was over. The audience continued to roar in ultimate satisfaction.

"The ancestors have come to us in the likeness of masquerades".

People began dispersing soon after the drummers left. Some even ran off with the masquerade. The crowd grew thinner and thinner. Soon, it was obvious that the ceremony was completely and finally over. The time then was 5:47 a.m.

Most activities and ceremonies of the Africans last through the night until the wee hours of the morning. This is essential to allow the ancestors ample time to emanate, interact, commune, and partake with the living and then depart. Because of the emotional attachment to these visitors from the underworld, people do not feel the need to sleep. In fact, it is as soon as the masquerades leave the arena that people begin to feel sleepy, tired, and the desire to go home.

It is interesting also to note that when the dancers perform, spectators throw money on them as a show of appreciation and support. The money is often allowed to touch the floor before it is picked up---a symbolic gesture honoring Mother Earth as the source of all wealth, fertility, reproduction, fecundity, and life, from whom all humankind came and to whom all humankind shall return.

CHAPTER 5

The Rituals of Identity

Different regions of Africa have different family types. Family life in Africa varies from region to region and from ethic group to ethnic group. Despite their diversity, Africans have much in common. They share many cultural characteristics and core values. These include respect for the elderly, parents and grandparents, strong loyalty to their clans, communities, and families.

Most importantly, they share a strong family tie. Africans cherish their children. No matter how poor, each African family seeks the best for its children and feels a strong sense of responsibility for their education and welfare. In Africa, no one is ever alone.

Elderly parents and grandparents are cared for and supported throughout life. When a child's parents die, the child is taken into the family of an aunt or an uncle. When a woman loses her husband in death, the woman is jointly cared for by her husband's family. She also has an option of returning to her parents. After graduation from high school or college, an African boy or girl going to the city to find employment knocks at the door of an uncle, an aunt, a third or fourth cousin, or a distant relative he has never seen.

They all share a common cultural heritage that is influenced by their belief in the existence of their ancestors; thus, the general cultural elements of the African can be discussed collectively in this volume.

Despite their regional differences and acculturation, Africans in America are united in the high value they place on home, family, and kin. For an African, the extended family is a strong source of support, which, in the dominant culture, may be sought outside the family. They rely on their family for counsel through all vicissitudes of life.

Disputes and misunderstanding among couples, parents, and their children are settled in the family by elders, as it is done in their home land. They depend on each other for babysitting and child care advice.

World View

One of the core elements that bind the Africans together is their common worldview. This worldview is based on their strong belief in God whom they worship in many different ways and in the existence of ancestors. Although many immigrant African families are Christians, they still share the same core values.

They believe that God created all things. However, it is the concept of "reaching" Him that makes their traditional religion different from the Christian religion. One of the immigrants explained: "We Africans have complete belief in God.

You can see that from the names we give to our children, and from our way of life." He went on to explain that most Africans do not understand the concept of statues used for worship. He expressed his feelings in a very direct language:

> When the missionaries came, they got us to believe in their God, but destroyed our statues and called them idols. Now, I've come to America, and I've found that they, too, have statues. If I walk into the church now and break or burn the statue of Virgin Mary or St. Joseph, they will accuse me of sacrilege. They will put me in jail. It is the same thing. St. Joseph is a saint. His status as a saint is not different from the status of my grandfather as an ancestor. They call ours ancestral worship. What then will I call their practice? We all are looking for answers to this phenomenon.

Family Core Values

African immigrants in America vary in their hold on their traditional African values. Most African immigrants still believe in the traditional concept of the father as head of the household, making decisions that affect the family, running the affairs of the household, and receiving the utmost respect. In some households, the father's traditional influence is dwindling. Other aspects of the immigrant African family values that are affected by this transition are discussed in the following pages.

Familism

Familism refers to the centrality of the family (Friedman, 1998). As stated earlier Africans believe in the importance and centrality of the family. An African would normally not get married without the consent and blessing of his or her parents. Most Africans in America would travel many miles home to get a wife because they want their families to be a part of the marriage. Even when they found each other here in America, the man and the woman would still need to go home and show themselves to their families for approval.

However, due to distance and financial constraints, too many people no longer take this loyalty trip home. There are others who do not worry about this aspect of the culture. They simply "live their lives."

Filial Piety

In African families, children are taught to respect not only their parents, but also their grandparents and other elders who are not members of the family. Filial piety, which prescribes that children should repay their parents' love and care by caring for them in their old age (Friedman, 1998), is a highly cherished family value. Africans exhibit this worthy value by inviting their parents to live with them at their old age. They would provide for them and care for them for the rest of their lives.

Africans in America also reflect this value by sponsoring their parents to come to the United States. Many African parents and grandparents have visited the United States at one time or another in their lives, more than any other time in history. They do not only come to experience the wonder that is America, they also come to see their children and grandchildren; those they have not been able to see in years. You could read in the eyes and faces of these grandparents the fulfillment of life itself and the realization of a dream that otherwise would have been virtually impossible.

Respect for the Elderly

As an extension of Filial Piety, respect for the elderly does not stop with parents, grandparents, and other elderly persons that are living; it also extends to the elderly persons that are dead. Thus, one finds Africans according their ancestors great respect at all times. Because older persons in the village have emerged victorious from all the battles of life and are now ready to transcend the pathos of mortality, they command the respect of everyone in the community.

They are automatically elevated to the status of "Father of All," and are treated as such by all. Everyone takes care of them and buys them gifts. African immigrants in America still honor old age. They express respect for this highly cherished institution by taking gifts with them as they go home to visit regardless of the distance and excess luggage fees.

When these aged fathers die and become ancestors, they continue to receive gifts and respect from the living. This practice is evident in their rituals and celebrations when they present their ancestors with food and drink, thanking them for their presence and protection and soliciting their help in times of difficulty. They speak well of them regardless of their situation. They present them with the freshest palm wine, food, and kolanut.

The immigrants have continued to practice this value. During their meetings and ceremonies, they serve kolanut or any other cultural symbol to the elderly persons first before the others. It is also the eldest among them that performs the ritual of libation and kolanut. This value could also be found among the children of the immigrants. They call every grown African male "Uncle" and every grown African female "Auntie."

Respect for Authority

Traditional African values also emphasize respect for authority. Children are taught early in life to obey the rules of the land and respect all authority. At school, students' duties include respect and obedience for teachers. Students would not talk back to their teachers and would stand up as the teacher enters the classroom.

Usually, there would be a class monitor whose duty it is to strike the desk to alert everyone of the teacher's entry. Even in the absence of the teacher, students remain quiet and in their seats.

Traditionally, law enforcement agencies in Africa do not carry guns; they carry batons. In other words, people do not resist arrests or attempt to fight the police. Arrests are usually tranquil.

In America, due to pressure or sometimes greed, a few African immigrants have found themselves in trouble with the law. Some of them are in jail, and a few have visited the jailhouse at one time or another. Generally, African immigrants still hold this value dearly and are working hard to keep it.

"One Soiled Finger"

In Africa, when one family member loses face (does something wrong), it reflects on the rest of the family. A high value is placed, therefore, on maintaining self-respect and saving face. This family value is often expressed in their many proverbs, which include the following:

Otu aka ruta mmanu, ya ezuo oha **(When one finger is stained with oil, it spreads to all the fingers).**

Ihere anaghi eme onye ohi; o bu umu nna ya **(The shame is not on the thief, but on his relatives).**

Hence, when one loses face, his or her family members feel the embarrassment. Inappropriate behavior is not just a shame on the persons who

75

carried out the behavior, but on everybody who is related to him or her. It is a bad reflection on the family, for example, when a girl becomes pregnant while unmarried and living with her parents. She loses face and brings shame to herself, her parents, and her family. She is said to have desecrated the land, and her family must propitiate the land.

The consequences are enormous. The girl may end up not ever getting married and will live in her parents' household all her life. If a person commits a crime, that family is doomed because it always comes back to hunt the family in various family-oriented events. During marriage, for example, a family with a bad reputation or that has lost face would have difficulty finding a suitor for their daughters or finding a wife for their sons.

If any member of the family was found stealing, the entire family is doomed. The family will have difficulty associating freely with the rest of the community, and every female born in that family will have difficulty finding a husband.

In America, this value still seemed to hold strong. However, due to pressure of acculturation, few Africans tend to have forgotten this high family value and have had several occasions when they have lost face. They have become like the little bird *Nza* who forgot himself after a heavy meal and challenged his god.

Despite their incessant admonitions, the falcon still could not hear the falconer. Some African parents find their daughters having children outside wedlock.

The scandal and shame are still strong regardless of the transition. This act does not just bring shame to the parents and relatives here in America, but also to the family and relatives in Africa.

Fatalism

Fatalism, defined as the acceptance of one's fate (Friedman, 1998), is a strongly held belief in Africa. Africans believe strongly in predestination. They

76

believe that everyone's fate is inscribed in the palm of everyone's hand. Every one's inscription is unique and matches no other. Before a child is born, his or her destiny had been determined; hence no one lives beyond his destiny, and nothing happens to anyone that had not been predetermined.

Africans, therefore, learn to accept their fortune or misfortune as a mark of fate. They do not challenge an unfortunate event, but they accept it as the will of the Creator for the person. A pre-matured death is seen as the will of God and as a result of the person's destiny. It is a pragmatic way of coping with life's vicissitudes.

In America, the Africans seem to hold on strongly to this belief. During the period of this research, an illustrious African died. He was the president of the African Community Organization in Houston, Texas and had a successful business. When he was appointed the Assistant to the Governor of his home state in Nigeria, he gave up his business and went home to serve.

News came to the African community in Houston that he had died in a fatal car accident. What one speaker said echoed this belief in *fatalism*:

> *We are not going to sit hear and ponder why he had to go back home, or whether he would have lived had he stayed here. Whether he was here in America or there in Nigeria, what would have been would have been.*

Keeping the Dream Alive

African families generally place a high value on education. Traditionally, in many parts of Africa, education is not free from the time a child enters school. Students are required to bring all their supplies to school, ranging from pencils and erasers to books and tuition.

Most parents forfeit their personal enjoyment and welfare and are willing to undergo tremendous financial stress to assure that their children get good education. For example, most parents sponsored their children to America to obtain higher education.

While in America, Africans continue to uphold this value. They work odd shifts and keep two to three jobs to be able to pay their school fees. Most Africans today have doctoral and master's degrees. They are medical doctors, lawyers, engineers, nurses, physical and respiratory therapists, professors, teachers, administrators, and so on. An African in America would rather starve to have his children have a good start in education. Most of their children attend private and parochial schools where tuition is required than public schools without tuition.

"One Man, One Machete"

The traditional African family is patriarchal, the man is the head of the house. He maintains authority and has the responsibility to care and provide well for his wife and children. Male children are more valued than female, and men could go any length to have a son. Some men marry second and third wives in "search" of a male child.

The oldest male is a very important part of the family. He is looked upon as the heir to carry the touch of the family when the father goes to be with his Maker. He commands the respect of his siblings and other family members.

The mother's role is to nurture and care for the family, including her husband. She has the responsibility of teaching the younger children. She is traditionally the cook of the family, making sure that there is food enough for everyone.

The children's role is obedience and respect. The girls stay with their mother and learn how to cook, how to make their husbands happy, and other household maintenance skills, while the boys stay with their fathers and learn how to carry out the masculine chores.

Everyone helps in the raising of children, including adults who are not immediate family members, because, as they say in Africa, it takes a village to raise a child. Parents would leave their children at home and go to work. The children would know to go to anybody's compound to play with the other children. They would know to come home to each lunch. Sometimes, the mothers of the children with whom they were spending the day would feed them.

Perhaps the most important lessons taught to children are obedience and respect for age and authority. Through story telling, songs, and experiences, children learn moral values, honor, and duty.

The traditional African family is often patrilocal, with the married couple living in the same household with the husband's parents. Even when they relocate and move to cities for employment, they all usually come home to the same household during holidays or during festivals.

Sometimes, the husband stays away in the city while his wife and children stay at home with his parents. Children do not traditionally separate from their families. As they grow up and get married, their families become extensions of the original unit.

"Things Fall Apart"

A major issue with the African family in America is the problem of control and gender role. Women emancipation and generational conflicts tend to reduce the authority of the man as the head of the household; thus, the African family in America is beginning to feel the heat of this transition. Acculturation, pressure, and interface with American culture have caused many African families to disintegrate.

Conflicts arise between spouses and between parents and children. As more and more families depend on two breadwinners, women income becomes critical to the family's survival. Some women find themselves working until their last months of pregnancy. If they should be on bed rest for a long time, the family suffers.

As African women begin to work outside the home and bring more money home, they become more westernized in their attitude toward money and authority, and they consequently begin to challenge their husbands' authority and dominance as the head of the household. Working educated African women have

79

begun to express a need for equality in the family, especially as they are exposed to American mores and values.

Generally, traditional male/female roles are changing. As women take advantage of educational opportunities and find gainful employment, their self-image change, and they begin to seek freedom and even authority.

Traditionally, refusal of meal by a husband was an indication that the man was unhappy with his wife. Therefore, when a man "refused" her wife's food, she would do whatever it took to make it up. In America, when a husband would refuse food, his wife would put it back into the refrigerator and would eat it later.

Some African immigrant families are gradually becoming matriarchal. Mothers are assuming the role of the head of the household. The reason perhaps is due largely to the interface with the values of the dominant culture, or perhaps seeking the best of both worlds. When parents divorce or separate, the children stay with the mother, rather than with the father, as prescribed by traditional African custom.

During a gathering of one of the African immigrant groups in 1997, its president lamented on the decadence of the African family structure due to cultural transition. Part of his address states:

> *Our institution of marriage is another fabric of our culture that has suffered a great setback, particularly here in the United States. The failure to adhere to our long-cherished marriage traditions has resulted to violence in the homes, instabilities in families, frequent police presence in the homes, and eventual disintegration of families. It is disheartening to note that the rate of divorce among our people is approaching alarming proportions. This is partly due to the absence of certain cultural mechanisms that could have been applied to address family problems. This problem is exacerbated by misconceptions about rights of equality in the family. In as much as both husband and wife share equal rights, the cultural norm places greater responsibility on the man for the welfare of the family.*

The truth of the matter is that African men are very particular about their place in the family. Stepping on those toes prick on dangerous nerves and cause troubled reactions. When women neglect their place and the place of their husbands in the family, they begin to challenge the natural role and authority of the African man. At that point, in the eyes of the African man, the woman becomes man. One thing that the African man does not do, according to one of the s, is marry his fellow man.

In spite of this conflict, some African households still remain husband-headed, and women still find time to cook. They still prefer homemade foods to pre-prepared foods in the grocery stores. Stewed rice, plantain, soup for *fufu* and *amala, and yam* are still the popular staple among the African immigrants.

"No Longer At Ease"

When the immigrant African children and youth attend schools, they are taught different values and beliefs, and they bring this home to their parents' chagrin and shock. Children no longer grow up in a communal setting as did their parents, and this has become a major issue in family discussions, to find a way of getting the children to seek out their own and to rekindle that fire of community in their children.

Most African parents now send their teenage children home to experience the real culture first hand, and learn the truth through interaction with people at home. Some of these children come back with significant changes in attitude and behavior.

Generally, the minds of most African immigrant parents are no longer at ease. They shiver in the thought that they might lose their children. Most have sought the face of God for intervention in what would otherwise become a disastrous situation. Most of them now attend churches regularly, belong to different Christian organizations, and spend time with their children as much as their work schedules would permit. In some cases, the results are uplifting.

CHAPTER 6

Symbols of Identity

Among the Africans, communication is the root of all socialization and enculturation process. They communicate, among other things, through art, music, and dance. Africans have a rich tradition of oral literature, which has been the most common form of enculturation. Through oral tradition, cultural traits, values, and norms are passed on from generation to generation.

The literature includes histories of ethnic and kinship groups, legends or cultural heroes. It also includes stories of tricksters, animal fables, proverbs, riddles, and songs of praise for the chiefs, kings, and wrestling heroes.

Auditory Communication Patterns

Story Telling

Story telling is a very powerful communication tool among Africans. Folk tales are used to teach moral, decency, good behavior, etiquette, roles, and a host of other values. The best stories are told by old men, men who had been warriors in their time, the soon would-be ancestors, the custodians of morality and values, the living libraries of people who had no books.

They told stories of different kinds, tales about life and death, of good and evil. Some of the tales cause their audience to tremble with excitement; some held the listeners spellbound in rapt fascination.

Proverbs

Proverbs, as the Africans say, are the palm oil with which words are eaten. Different regions have different proverbs associated with their language. The proverbs have deeper meanings and explain matters more completely. Proverbs are called wise sayings, because they contain information that counsel, reprimand, and advise without expending much energy.

Music

Music is very important in the life of the African. It is a powerful means of communication and of passing on information from generation to generation. Newborn babies listen to their mothers' and older siblings as they sing to them. As the children listen, they learn about life, about moral, about right and wrong, about the members of the family, and about important people and events of the community, tribe, and country (Dietz and Olatunji, 1965).

Drums

Africans beat drums during ceremonies, including birth, death, initiation ceremonies, and famous events. Talking drums, especially, have a tonal ability to duplicate African speech. They are used to disseminate information across the village.

Talking drums imitate the pitch of the human voice (Dietz and Olatunji, 1965), and it is used to pour encomiums on a king, or sing the praises of a warrior. They are also used to announce the deaths of heroes, warriors, and kings. Among the Ashanti of Ghana and the Yoruba of Nigeria, for example, talking drums can transmit tones of vowels, and their beats correspond to spoken sentences or phrases (Junior League of Houston, 1995).

Visual Communication Patterns
Gestures

Gesture is used very powerfully by Africans to communicate to one another. Body movement, facial expressions, and hand signals play important roles in the African cultural communication system. For instance, a mother may wink at her children if she wants them to leave the area immediately, or to be quiet.

In the traditional African society, left-handedness was considered a bad sign. In Senegal and Nigeria, for example, it is considered bad manners to eat with the left hand (The Junior League of Houston, 1995), give or receive with a left hand, or shake someone's hand using the left hand.

Africans use different ways to communicate goodwill and welcome. In some parts of Africa, among the Igbo of Nigeria, for instance, guests know that they are welcome when they are presented with kolanut by the host.

Clothing

In Africa, mourners wear black clothes to communicate their grief and loss. Although no words are exchanged, one readily identifies a mourner in the midst of everyone else.

Certain attires communicate certain roles and missions. There are different outfits worn by the medicine men during rituals and by the village chiefs during celebrations.

Tender Palm Fronds

When tied around a particular area, tender palm fronds communicate restriction. During masquerade performances, tender palm fronds are used to demarcate the spectators' area from the performance arena. It also communicates to the masquerader that the spectators are not participant observers, but side viewers.

Home Cooking

In African families, food plays a vital role in maintaining cohesive identity, and home cooking is a symbol of womanhood. Like everyone, Africans love to eat.

Traditionally, mealtime is a time for families to come together and eat together. The women are enthusiastic cooks, and they cook the meal with the freshest ingredients obtained from their gardens and farms. Most of these ingredients are grown in the compound.

African immigrants to America come from different regions of the continent. Despite their busy schedule, the immigrants attempt to recreate a taste of Africa and to introduce their children to their traditional foods by cooking at home and preparing meals similar to those that they eat at home. As they come together and celebrate together, they discover the similarities and differences in their fellow immigrants' foods (Cook and Belanus, 1997).

Several years ago, there were no stores where immigrants could buy African foods or ingredients to make their own food. Today, ingredients for authentic African foods could be found in African grocery stores all around the United States.

Different types of African staples, for instance, plantain, which is one major contribution to African diet, are found in almost all African food stores in the United States. The plantain may be eaten green or ripe. It can also be fried, baked, boiled, or roasted and served either whole or in slices with pepper and red palm oil or other forms of healthy mixed vegetables. Plantain leaves are traditionally used to wrap up foods to be boiled or baked, for example *mahi-mahi, agidi, alibo*, etc.

In the Houston area, for instance, one could find African grocery stores in almost every neighborhood, each selling authentic African foods and spices. Mortar and pestle are used to grind some of these spices and ingredients for food, and they are found in every traditional African kitchen. Most African food stores stock and sell full-size and miniature mortars and pestles as a reminder of the real home cooking.

Immigrants who own homes and have yard spaces grow their own home vegetables. They bring the seeds directly from home. Sometimes those who do not have access to seeds from home get some from their friend who do.

Many African food taboos are broken by this transition. In Africa, women are not supposed to eat kidney and gizzards from chicken and goat heads. They are reserved for the men. Now, women can buy, cook, and eat any animal part they choose and have craving for.

An immigrant woman confessed how she fantasized about the taste of the goat head as a child in her homeland, but she could taste it because only the men were allowed to it. In America, she now has a total declaration of independence, and she could buy the goat head, prepare it to her taste, and eat it without reservation (Cook and Belanus, 1997).

Like African food stores, African restaurants are propping up all around America, serving authentic African foods. Some combine African and Caribbean cuisines and cater to people from Brazil and other adventurous culinary ethnic groups. When too busy to sit down and cook traditional-style African meal, people usually treat themselves to their taste of home in these restaurants.

These restaurants also are invited to cater weddings, naming ceremonies, and even when dignitaries visit from home. In the Houston and Dallas areas, visitors to every African festival are treated to authentic African foods. In Washington, D. C., African foods are served at every major rite of passage, including birth, marriage, and death (Cook and Belanus, 1999).

Audacious Ventures

Many African immigrants have been successful in opening their own businesses and making their marks in the society. In addition to restaurant and grocery businesses, Africans have also been very successful in other businesses, including dressmaking, hair braiding, cab driving, home health, gas stations, and so on.

Africans have teachers in American public schools and professor in American universities and colleges. African physicians, lawyers, engineers, architects, Real Estate brokers, and accountants serve both the African and the American population and have their own offices all over the country.

African immigrant newspapers could be found on counters in African grocery stores and other business offices. In the Houston area alone, for example, there is a barrage of newspapers and magazines published by African immigrants. The "USAfrica", "The Punch", "The international Guardian," and "The African News Digest," are just a few.

African immigrants also host many radio station talk shows and broadcast programs, providing entertainment, information, and home news to Africans in America. African immigrants have also climbed the political ladder. In the city of Cleveland in East Texas, for example, an African immigrant is Mayor. Recently, in the city of Houston, an African immigrant, Bernard Amadi, ran for a city council position, becoming the first African immigrant to run for such position in Houston.

Birth

Among the Africans, children are at the center of family life. The birth of a child brings joy and happiness to every African family and community. The birth of a boy brings a special joy because a boy will keep the name of the family.

When a girl is born, the parents are excited because a girl brings wealth, bride wealth; that is. African parents, grandparents, other siblings, and family members respond to newborn babies in very indulgent, affectionate ways.

In traditional Africa, most births take place at home. Family members, neighbors, and local midwives usually assist the mother during childbirth. The father is usually not allowed to witness the labor or the birth. When the baby is born and washed, the women explode in a chant to announce the arrival of the baby.

As soon the chant rings, every woman responds and makes her way to the home of the family. They would sing and dance and spray powder and white local chalk on their faces and their necks to show that they had been there. It is also a sign to others they would pass by on their way home to know that a baby has been born.

The mother is pampered. She is not allowed to do any chores. Family members far and near, come to assist the new mother. They would do all the cooking for the family and even feed the mother. They would wash the baby, feed the baby, and, at the same time, care for the other siblings. This assistance continues until the mother is strong enough to take care of herself.

Usually, the father selects the name for the child. Names are carefully chosen according to how the father would like the child to grow up. Names are also chosen according to events that surround the child's birth or took place during the birth of the child. Most African names reflect their believe in the power and goodness of God Almighty.

The pressure in America has continued to nibble on this rich cultural heritage. However, most Africans, in spite of their busy schedules, still continue to honor this beautiful age-old tradition. They make out time to visit a new mother, bring home-cooked food, and help with some household chores. Due to work schedule and other necessities, the mother's recuperation period is not as long as it is in Africa.

The baby makes early visit to the Day care center. Most parents sponsor their mothers to the United States to help with the care of the baby. Traditionally, the raising of the children had been the job of the mother. However, this rigid demarcation of roles is declining rapidly. African immigrant fathers now share and enjoy the child care role in immigrant African families.

The baby's traditional naming ceremony or Christening brings families together to share the joy of new birth. They dance to the tune of their cultural music and enjoy the taste of their traditional foods.

Death and Burial

Africans are known to be exuberant and boisterous in their daily activities and interactions and during festivals and celebrations. Death sends a cloud of silence and envelopes this loquacity and excitement. It brings grief, pain, and sadness to every African.

When a person dies, every activity of the family seems to stop and silence descends on the compound. The fireplace is cold. Relatives and neighbors bring food, do family chores, and spend nights with the bereaved.

The period of mourning varies, depending on the age and status of the deceased. Traditionally, mourning for an elderly person, a would-be ancestor, lasts as long as a year. During this time, the elder's wife is not allowed to go to the farm, market, or participate in any events of the village. Her hair is shaved or left untidy, and she wears black mourning clothes all through the duration of the mourning.

On the day of the burial, the whole village gathers, singing songs, and dancing. The women carry a photograph of the dead singing and dancing all across the village and neighboring towns. Usually, in some areas, it is the deceased first daughter who bears the picture on her head. When the gravediggers finish their job, the body is lowered amid wailing, crying, and screaming. Food and drinks are served enough for everyone present.

In America, death still has the same devastating impact on all Africans. America allows certain number of days for immediate family members to bury their dead and return to work, but this does not stop the African from paying the utmost respect due the dead. They would take time off work to make sure that their dead doesn't feel dejected as it makes its way to the world beyond.

Usually, they would announce a wake keeping, and everyone comes together and makes monetary contributions enough to send the body to its homeland. Usually, people's generous donations are enough to pay for the deceased spouse or closest relative to accompany the body.

Visitations to the family of the deceased continue for several weeks and even months. People bring food and drinks and also help out with household chores. This is one aspect of their life that has not been deeply affected by this transition.

The African Christian Fellowship (ACF) is a Christian organization that has chapters all over the United States. When a member dies, the members gather at the house of the bereaved and hold fellowship every night until the body of the deceased goes home. They make sure that food and drinks are in abundant supply all through the period and even beyond. They make sleepover schedules such that there are people in the house with the bereaved twenty-four hours a day, seven days a week.

During one of his speeches at the house of Brother Chima Osueke who died suddenly of a massive heart attack in Houston, Texas, the president of the Houston chapter of the ACF, Brother Ozougwu Aja, called on everyone to join the African Christian fellowship because the fellowship is for everyone and "membership has its privileges." In fact, membership does have its benefits. Many organizations do a lot to assist their bereaved member, but the African Christian Fellowship goes the extra mile.

When a member of the People's Club of Nigeria died in a car accident on a visit to his hometown, the organization pledged to provide food for one full year for his wife and children. This was in addition to a huge sum of money that was donated by the club to the family. The organization was also responsible for arranging for the wake keeping and the funeral, even though the accident did not occur in the United States.

In the early years of immigration, it was rare to hear about deaths among the African immigrants. Today, deaths are announced more frequently. A major cause of death among African immigrants is stress related, and the age range is between forty and fifty years old.

"The River Between"

The most devastating moments of the African Immigrant in America are those moments when news comes from home announcing the death of a family member. Most have grieved over the death of their fathers, mothers, sisters, brothers, uncles, aunts, grandparents, and so on and agonize more over the realization that they could not go home to see their dead bodies and could not do anything about it.

Due to distance, most people had not seen their parents or loved ones in more than six, seven, eight years and more. The distance, exacerbated by cost, makes the river between them deeper, darker, uncanny, more sinister, more ominous, and more mysterious.

Marriage

In traditional Africa, marriage is a family affair, and parents play a very important role in choosing whom their children marry. If, for instance, a son finds someone and decides within himself to marry her, he must still seek his parents' approval. Once approved, the family then begins to make arrangements for the marriage to take place.

The man's family pays the bride price to the girl's parents. A bride price can be expensive, and this is why a man must be ready before he begins to think of marriage. Some things in life are free, but not someone's daughter, besides, payment of the bride price makes the marriage proper and official.

It soon becomes a thing of ridicule to the family when any portion of the bride price is left unpaid. Bride price is usually paid with money, cattle, goats, clothes, and many other items as demanded by custom. If the marriage breaks up, the bride's parents must return the bride price in full. Any children from the marriage would belong to the father.

Traditional weddings in Africa vary slightly from region to region, but the concept and basic rituals are similar. For example, in Rwanda, traditional wedding is called *Kurongora* and *Igbankwu* among the Igbo of West Africa.

On the day of the traditional wedding, the groom and his family and friends go to the bride's house. There, they present their bride price to the parents. In some parts of Africa, it is customary to have the bride identify her husband by presenting him with a traditional drink. The real ceremony begins at this point. At the end of it all, the bride goes home with her husband.

In America, Africans still take marriage very seriously. A man who decides to get married still seeks the approval of his parents. Men usually travel home to find a wife. Even when they find their would-be wives in America, they still find time to take them home to show her to his parents.

The importance of marriage for the traditional African family cannot be overemphasized. Parents pray that their daughters keep themselves pure so that they could get a good husband. Sex before marriage is very uncommon and socially unacceptable. Children who are born outside wedlock are socially stigmatized and are not treated with as much respect as those born in wedlock.

African immigrant parents who have marriage-age daughters experience shock when they discover that they are the ones to sponsor the wedding of their daughter, especially in situations where their daughter is engaged to an American. Also, due to financial constraints and conflict in schedules, couples no longer wait to be traditionally married before they begin to have children. It is no longer unusual to see children acting as ushers, flower girls, ring-bearers, groomsmen, and bridesmaids in their parents' wedding.

Divorce

In traditional African culture, divorce is a rare phenomenon. Married couples stay together all their lives. Marriage is a family affair, and it involves everybody in the village, including distant relatives and even the dead. One of the immigrants puts it this way:

> *Every one of these people witnessed the wedding. While libation was being poured, the ancestors were also invited. To get a divorce, therefore, everyone present at the marriage ceremony has to be present for the divorce. Some of them may be dead. A man who divorces without the consent of the ancestors deprives himself of the protection of the ancestors.*

In America, the center doesn't seem to hold any longer, and things seem to have fallen apart. Divorce is rampant among African immigrants. Pressure and stress contribute to the degeneration of African immigrant family. Perhaps, as one of them pointed out, "people need to revisit their customs and traditions and touch bases with their roots. Otherwise, with the rate things are going, I'm afraid that many more families will break up before you know it."

Religion

Traditionally, African religion is highly organized and is intended to mediate between the human beings and natural and supernatural forces. It defines relationships between human beings and nature and between the young and the old. It gives reasons for human suffering and provides instruction on how to live a good life.

Many Africans still practice local traditional religions. Africans believe in a high God who dwells in the heavens, the creator of the universe and the source of all things good. They also believe that everything around them has spirits, and these spirits must be respected. When human beings die, their spirits are honored as ancestors. For them, religion functions as a search for meaning and deals with the nature of life and death.

Religion also functions to maintain social order and to reduce anxiety and fear of the unknown. This belief is expressed in symbols and myths and practiced through rituals, prayers, and offerings.

When the Christian missionaries came to Africa in the beginning in the nineteenth century, they brought a different form of belief and converted many people to Christianity. Although some Africans still maintain their traditional ways of worship, most of them today are Muslims, Catholics, Protestants, and other Christian denominations.

Most African Christians often keep some of their old beliefs along with the new ones. In recent years, the Christian churches have endeavored to work out a synthesis of Christian ethics and traditional African values; thus many denominations incorporate dancing in their worship services and allow members to dance down the aisle to bring forward their offerings.

94

Most African immigrants to America are Christians and Muslims. There are others among them who have maintained their traditional beliefs and forms of worship. Away from their native lands, they draw strength from their religious beliefs to help them create a framework for interpreting events and experiences and to meet their spiritual and secular needs.

Many African churches have mushroomed all over the United States. As one worshipper puts it, " It feels much better to be in your own environment, with your own people. The experience is different."

In the Houston area alone, there are over eighty different churches owned and operated by African immigrants. A few of them include the Amazing Grace Four-Square Gospel Church, His master's Vessel Ministries, The First African Baptist Church, The Chapel of Praise Ministries, the Redeemed Church of Christ, the Cherubim and Seraphim Congregation, and the list continues. Area mosques also abound which serves the Muslim population.

Cultural Patterning of Time

Perception of time differs in different cultures. Africans have a more flexible attitude toward time. Being punctual to events, festivals, and celebrations is not an important moral value.

Time, to them, is a human invention; hence, their natural tendencies to time influence their behavior; hence, they control time rather than being controlled by time. Listening for the rooster's crow in the mornings and watching the sun go down in the evenings have patterned their timing and contributed immensely to their response to events.

When they gather for their festivals and cultural events, there is no rush. They relax and take their time, knowing that the event will last till the wee hours of the morning. Most of their events do. Any event scheduled for 7:00 p.m. does not usually start until two or three hours later.

Most of the time, their invited American friends leave before the real thing starts. Most celebrants have learned to make separate invitations with different times for their friends who are not Africans. Overall, this time concept has not affected their professional experiences in America.

A Generation Displaced

When they first came, their initial idea was to get education, work, make money, and return to their native land. But for most of them, this has not been the case. When they left their countries, they forfeited everything. They came to America to make their dreams true.

For some of them, things didn't work out quite as planned in America. The dream seemed distant. They lost their place in their homelands and couldn't find a place in their new land. They faced tumultuous situations: shattered dreams, broken relationships, unemployment, economic hardship, and health problems. Their world seems to tumble before their eyes.

The countries they left behind didn't get any better. They stayed and waited for things to get better for them to return. The more they waited and hoped, the more ugly the situation became. Stories of economic disaster, extreme poverty, war, and human rights violations, deterred them from making the move. Most of them dared the consequences and went back home, bur their stories discouraged the rest to follow. They stayed in America.

Having spent so many years in a foreign land, they became accustomed to the fast life in America, and everything at home became too slow for them. They could no longer fit in the system in their countries. Their age mates and school mates who did not have the opportunity to come to America made their lives in their home countries, established there and took possession of everything that the *Tokunbos* had left behind. They had big houses and drove nice cars, while those in America had nothing and depended on them for "rides and good time."

When they return, they are introduced as "visitors from America." Surely, they had lost their place in history, and have become a generation displaced. They now sit by the rivers of Babylon and weep when they remember their Zion.

Although most of them are American citizens, their song tells where their hearts are:

O my home! O my home!
When shall I see my home
When shall I see my native land? I'll never forget my home.

"Weep Not, Child"

Although the traditional family role of male and female are drastically changing within the African immigrant families, the ideals the father and mother are still expressed and maintained. They tend to take a more bicultural stance, becoming Americans, while also trying to hold on to their cultural heritage as Africans.

Enculturation, passing on their culture to their children, is becoming more and more important to most African immigrants. Most African children are reared in close knit family units, which cause them to develop a mutual dependence upon their family and a collectivistic approach to life. As they grow and go away to colleges in various parts of the country, they are exposed completely to the mainstream culture. They soon begin to find many of the African customs and traditions to be too rigid for them. Some even begin to experience great stress while others rebel and reject their traditional African cultural values.

According to Aluko and Sherblom (1997), parents are concerned that their American-born children will grow up to be part of the melting pot of dominant culture. They are afraid that their children would grow up not knowing who they are. They have, therefore, actively redefined their ideas of tradition and community by recreating institutions and events that draw on expressive African forms. They have established language and culture schools where their children come together to celebrate their culture (N'Diaye, 1997).

A Lost Generation

For most African immigrant families, the process of enculturation has been very slow and lopsided. Participating in cultural activities alone would not do it. Experts in language would agree that language sustains culture. Unfortunately, only a small percentage of children of African immigrants understand or speak their parents' native language. A high percentage of African immigrant parents do not speak their native languages to their children at home, and this has been a concern to most cultural-minded Africans.

Although they engage in festivals and cultural celebrations as methods of enculturation, it would definitely be more meaningful to maintain a strong linguistic tie in order to effectively transmit their cultural heritage to their American-born children. Would once-a-month cultural gathering make a difference in the lives of these children or would these children of a displaced generation themselves become a lost generation? Only time will tell.

CHAPTER 7

African World View: The Case of the Igbo

Africans are proud of their artistic heritage. The place of the artist in the society speaks volume about the position art occupies in the life of the people. In fact, to understand African culture more fully, one has to understand its art.

When the immigrants first came to America, they did not bring their art forms with them. However, they brought their talents and expertise. Today, African art is continuously making its way into the United States. It could be found in galleries, museums, and homes across the nation. Many people, especially educators, are beginning to pay particular attention to African art. They have continued to express their interest and appreciation for this form of art and have begun to value its role in the making of a great culture.

African art originates from particular circumstances, historical and cultural. To best understand it therefore, attention must be paid to the concepts and the values that surround its creation. African art functions at different levels, and one must understand these different levels, the root of the work, and the role of the work of art in the society.

African art is conceptual. It represents ideas drawn from the philosophy of their worldview. It is interwoven with the daily life of the people in ways quite different from most Western art. Religious beliefs find artistic expression not only in the masks and figures created primarily for ceremonial purposes, but in the practical objects of day-to-day existence.

Tribal religion is very common in Africa. Its core is ancestral worship. This reflects the people's concept of the cosmos (Universal belief). It interprets the people's belief system or worldview. The tribal society realizes that there is

99

cosmic rhythm operating on different levels other than its own. Cosmic rhythm can be called the generating forces because they contain life forces or vital forces, the vital energy, which controls all forms of social institutions including procreation.

Survival of a tribal society depends upon its ability to harness power from the vital energy or force, and African art serves as a means of tapping power from this vital energy (the supernatural). This could be done by way of sacrifices. Vital energy could be good or bad, hence there are benevolent and malevolent spirits.

Symbolism is another characteristic of African tribal religion. Religion itself is coming into terms with the vital force --- seeking peace with the Almighty. Work of art provides the means for this relationship.

African art can be classified into two major groups --- man-regarding and spirit-regarding. For example, in Nigeria, man-regarding art is found among the Yoruba and the Benin where art is used to honor the ruling monarch and adorn the palace. It is materialistically embellished to portray the power, wealth and grandeur of the monarch or patron and gears toward naturalism and realism. Some of the Baroque and Renaissance portraits and sculptures could be classified in this category.

Spirit-regarding art is found among the Igbo of Nigeria where art is used to tap power from the ancestors and the supernatural forces. There is therefore an extreme abstraction, a conscious distortion of proportion in order to achieve the image of a spirit. In the areas where art is man- regarding, there is always a central authority among the people. In the areas where art is spirit-regarding, there is no central authority. The following pages will focus on the cultural context of the art of the Igbo of West Africa --- the spirit-regarding art.

Masters of their Environment

When the Europeans found their way into West Africa between the 16th and 19th centuries, the art of most West African countries suffered, especially

100

those in the riverine areas. In Nigeria, for example, many art objects were taken by force and shipped to Britain. Since then, to the Europeans and most of the world, the art of Western Nigeria has seemed to epitomize the art of Africa.

Yet, faced with the same pressure of missionary invasion and foreign influence, the art of the Igbo in the Eastern part of the country, which is essentially spirit-regarding, thrived and survived. It was not simply because the Igbo is in the hinterland and could not be reached by the Europeans, but mainly because the Igbo are the masters of their environment, a powerful tribe bound and protected by powerful ancestors; hence their culture has remained pristine and their art sacrosanct over the years and through the ages.

Unlike their neighboring tribes, the Yoruba, Fulani, Hausa and Benin, who expanded into large empires and dynasties by conquering other tribes and states, the Igbo neither expanded into a large empire nor conquered by their neighbors. Even the Fulani Jihad of the 19th Century, which swept through most African cities and states, did not sweep through Igboland. Their survival amid all the turbulence and ravaging wars still remains a mystery to all. Little wonder their neighbors still stand in internal awe of them.

The Igbo create different types of art, ranging from disposable baskets to the most durable pottery and sculpture pieces. Their art includes the cloth weaving of Akwette, the pottery of Ishiagu, the basketry of Otampa, the metalsmithing of Awka, the masks and wood figures of Nsukka, Onitsha, and Afikpo, the bronze sculptures and terra-cotta heads of Igbo-Ukwu, all of which date as far back as the tribe itself.

For example, the oldest pottery found is from the early fourth millennium B. C. E. (Sieber, 1980). Some of these art pieces serve decorative purposes; others serve religious and ritualistic purposes. Pottery vessels, for example, are used in rituals, placed in shrines and buried in graves.

An attempt has been made to limit the scope of this study for purposes of clarity and efficacy. Although the Igbo create different types of art, using different materials which include ivory, stone, raffia and plant fibers among a host

101

of others, it is the mask carving among the Igbo which will be examined in this study because it is the most important aspect of their art, and because, as Schmalenbach (1988) also observes, the traditional tribal art of Africa is primarily sculpture in wood.

It should also be noted that Igbo masks serve a great variety of purposes ranging from the simplest form of comedy and entertainment to the most complex and sophisticated religious ritual. However, this study will focus mainly on the religious and ritualistic aspect of the mask --- as a means of communication with the supernatural powers, as an abode of a spirit and as that which reaffirms the truth and immediate presence of myths in everyday life.

The perspective assumed in this study is entirely religious and ritualistic. This is necessary because the art of the Igbo described in this study --- the mask carving --- is essentially spirit-regarding. Since the art of some parts of Africa are man-regarding, some of the views shared here may not apply directly to such specific works of art. However, despite this slight difference, the basic concept of all African wood sculpture is the same --- religious and ritualistic.

In these areas where works of art are created to honor the kings and beautify the palace, the kings are regarded as godheads or as representatives of God on earth; hence religion and ritual also apply. Apart from the aforementioned, the researcher does not foresee any serious problem with generalizability.

The Igbo World

The Igbo, over eight million, occupy the present Anambra, Enugu, Abia, Imo, and Ebonyi States of Nigeria. They are the largest ethnic group of Eastern Nigeria and consist of multitudes of villages. They are a warlike people united by a unilateral ancestry and protected by powerful ancestors. They are believed to have occupied their land since prehistoric times.

Igbo world is a vast world, a wondrous world, a whispering world, enigmatic but dynamic, both in spatial and temporal realms. Its culture is like *oke ohia* (a big jungle), *anaghi epiocha ya epiocha* (inexhaustible).

The origin of the Igbo was initially located at the confluence of the Niger and Benue Rivers. The first Igbo in the region may have moved onto the Awka-Orlu plateau between four and five thousand years ago. It is interesting to note that originally, the Igbo shared linguistic ties with the Bini, Igala, Yoruba, and Idoma.

The split between them occurred probably between five and six thousand years ago (Arts & Life of Africa Online). Some traces of the original similarities may still exist today. For example, the Yoruba phrase *E je ka lo*, which means, "Let's go," has a similar shade in spelling and meaning with the Igbo version, *E je alo, which means "Go well," or "Safe journey."*

Most Igbo are subsistent farmers, and their main crops include yams, cassava, coco yam, palm oil, and corn. The harvesting of yam (the king of crops) is a time for celebration. Yam is usually eaten with palm oil, made from the fruit of the palm tree, which is processed into palm oil.

Their culture places a great deal of emphasis on self-reliance, equality, democracy, and a strong competition for social, economic, and political advancement. Tribal associations are common and include title societies, age-grades and men's secret societies.

The Igbo calendar is separated into seven four-day weeks (28 days) and forms the basic cycle for the masked rituals of each village's secret society. For the Igbo, the number seven is a significant number. It implies completeness. Perhaps this concept of the number seven has its roots from the biblical significance of the number, referencing the seven plagues in Egypt; Naaman's cleansing after the seventh plunge into the river, Jesus' feeding of the multitude (five loaves and two fish equal seven), God resting on the seventh day, forgiving your neighbor seventy times seven, and so on. It is this secret society with which the Igbo masks are directly associated, and through which the masked rites occur.

All male members of the village are expected to join the society by the time they are adults---many become members as children. Women, uninitiated boys and men are excluded. The initiation rites and certain titles remain secrets, however, masquerades, which form one of its principle activities, are generally held in public.

The Igbo are a politically fragmented group. The Igbo resist central authority, and have centralized chieftaincy, hereditary aristocracy or kingship customs, as can be found among their neighbors. Decisions are made unanimously by the *Umu nna,* an assembly of elders, village councils, which include the heads of lineages, elders, titled men, and men who have established themselves economically within the community.

However, the priests of *Ala (*Mother Earth) and priests of *Ndi Ichie* (the Ancestors) share the real authority. If a man conducts himself very well and is ready to meet the *omenala* (the rules and demands of the land) entailed in acquiring rank, he could be initiated into the *Ozo* and could become the nominal leader of the council.

Igbo world is a unique world. Its language shares no resemblance nor spoken by any other people on the planet. The word "Igbo" is used in three senses: to refer to Igboland, to the indigenous speakers of the language, and to the language spoken by them.

Other major tribes in Nigeria share their languages with others outside the country. For instance, the Benin and the Yoruba who trace their origin to Oduduwa find traces of their dialect spoken in Ghana, former Dahomey, and Togo; hence a Yoruba person that moves to any of these territories could adjust easily.

Toward Northern Nigeria, one can hardly differentiate between persons from Hausa and Fulani and persons from Chad, Niger Republic, Senegal and even the rest of the Arab world. They share almost the same culture, the same religion, and the same language. Such circumstances trigger some curiosity as to why the Igbo are so distinct.

104

The Igbo are a proud people, tenacious in their belief, audacious in their venture, intense in their resistance, and suicidal in their persistence. They strive for excellence despite pressure from their neighbors. Their boldness, intelligence and refusal to be intimidated became a factor in the open antagonism against them, open hatred and alienation. None of the tribes could accept the Igbo, but they are bitterly aware that they cannot exist without the Igbo. There must have been a very strong reason why the Igbo lived the way they did and lived for so long amid such strong antagonism and opposition.

The Igbo is essentially a chiefless tribe. *"Igbo enwe eze"* (the Igbo have no king) is an old saying in Igboland. There is no central authority. There is a belief that democracy originated from Igboland even long before it came to Greece.

The Igbo, basically, pledge no allegiance to any chief. An Igbo who becomes a chief is still an ordinary person in the eyes of his fellow tribesmen, quite unlike the Yoruba and the Hausa who genuflect completely in obeisance before their Saudanas, Sultans, Emirs, Onis and Obas.

Chieftancy in Igboland was the creation of the British as a means of facilitating indirect rule. They had no problem ruling the other tribes, which they found in Nigeria because those tribes already had rulers. Their first attempt to create a chieftancy in Igboland---the Warrant Chiefs---was met with strong opposition from the women, which resulted in the first women's riot ever in Nigeria in 1929---the Akwette women's riot.

Today, the Igbo are beginning to make a mockery of the chieftancy title. There is a proliferation of such titles everywhere. Anybody can become a chief provided he can afford the financial demands. The irony is that chieftancy has become a title without respect. The traditional titles recognized in Igboland are the *Ofo* and the *Ozo* titles.

Means of living, therefore, is by tapping the ancestors through works of art. The ancestors live in the memory of their descendants and in the family ritual in which they receive regular invocations and daily offerings of food, drinks and kolanut. It is important to point out that the Igbo do not worship their ancestors; they honor them.

Cole and Aniakor (1984) note that men and ancestors protect and affect one another, a principle of reciprocity which demands that the ancestors be honored and offered regular sacrifice and they, in turn, prosper the lineage and protect its members. As Huet (1978) also observes, "the gods receive their power from the homage paid to them by men, and men in turn achieve prosperity through the force of the gods... a perpetuation of man-god alliance" (p. 29).

The Igbo communicate through prayer, sacrifice, symbol, music and dance, and their art plays a very important role in this worship and interaction. Achebe (1984) describes the Igbo world as "an arena for interplay of forces ... a dynamic world of movement and of flux" (p. ix). It consists of the human world and the world of the spirits---a world inhabited by people and things and the world of the Creator, the gods, the ancestors respectively.

It is a world of constant interaction between the physical world and the spiritual world, the visible and the invisible, the good and the bad, the living and the dead. They strive to appease all the gods of the land all the time and to meet the demands of all the forces that govern the land. As Achebe goes on to say, "it is this need and the striving to come to terms with a multitude of forces and demands which give Igbo life its tense and restless dynamism and its art an outward, social, and kinetic energy" (p. ix). Duerden (1971) describes the life force as an indefinite, indefinable power, which embraces all mystery, all secret power, and all divinity.

The art of the Igbo is functional. It is created to improve and reflect their dynamic interactions with the environment and their cultural ideas, the quality of life, to honor gods and to entertain. It serves as an instrument by which contacts are made with the supernatural forces. It helps them to overcome the fear of their environment, the fear of unseen forces.

Igbo art also serves as a means of expressing the inexpressible, of communicating with mysterious unseen powers, of penetrating into the true fabric

106

of things. As Schmalenbach (1988) notes, "these forces are directly perceived as everyday presences; they attend one's every movement, and all of this has a definite effect on the art produced to appease them" (p.14).

The Igbo artists carve their masks with inspired hands, scrupulously "translating into solid wood, the extraordinary shapes of abstract ideas" (Davidson, 1971, p. 151). When creating their art, they do not intend to exhibit it under the powerful lighting of the museum, nor are they concerned primarily with its aesthetic quality; their primary intention is always to create an abode for a spirit, because, as Graham-White (1974) observes, "the main purpose of the mask is to attract the spirit to the performer, rather than to display a representation of the spirit to the spectators" (p. 24). Hence, as Thompson (1974) also notes, "the artist is more influenced by the vital body in implied motion, by forms of flexibility, than by realism of anatomy per se" (p. 44).

This does not completely rule out the fact that the art of the Igbo could be viewed for its aesthetic quality; after all, Cubism, Pablo Picasso's brainchild, was inspired by African art. It is important to recall here that Igbo art is essentially spirit regarding, and the primary intention of the artist, therefore, is to erect a place where a spirit will reside. This intention is far removed from the artistic value ascribed to the work in the museum context.

This does not in any way suggest that the Igbo artist does not exhibit any aesthetic sensibility. He works to please an ancestor or a spirit, which is expected to honor the piece by establishing its presence in the finished work. The artist expresses satisfaction and speaks "beauty" only when the spirit accepts the work. As Schmalenbach (1988) observes, in the Igbo context, the aesthetic quality of a piece of art is not as important as its ritual efficacy. Therefore, no matter how "beautiful" a work may seem to appear in the eyes of the beholder, refusal by a spirit renders it inefficacious and "bad" and puts the artist back to work.

In the Igbo context therefore, a piece of art remains valuable as long as it is animated by this life-force. To understand the art of the Igbo, one must accept its intrinsic value --- the religious element that begets it, the vital energy that permeates it, and the practical function that it serves. It is then and only then that any form of appreciation will begin to occur. This practical function, says Achebe (1984), "is to channel a spiritual force into an aesthetically satisfying physical form that captures the presumed attribute of that force" (p. ix).

The Igbo Immigrant Group

The Igbo are a very gregarious and effervescent people, very vivacious and ebullient. Although they can be found all over the United States, their influence is strongly felt in Houston. Most of them occupy strategic positions in the city's workforce, and their children add to the rising percentage of African-Americans in Houston schools.

Many millions of miles away from their fatherland and having been exposed for a long time to social and cultural process of acculturation, they still realize the pressing and urgent need to preserve their cultural heritage. They still realize the need to educate their children in the culture of their people.

Through festivals, ceremonies and religious practices, they attempt to recreate and uphold the cultural rituals that adorn their ancestral land, and, as Mbabuike (1991) also observes, they attempt to ensure the survival of their traditional values and the unity of their tribe against the powerful gravitational pull of cultural and racial assimilation and the secularizing materialism of Western societies.

Houston has been home for hundreds of Igbo, most of who have been forced to stay away from their fatherland, longer than they had initially planned, due to the political instability and the deplorable economic situation of their country, Nigeria. Regular cultural activities become a *sine qua non* to maintain and protect their norms, values, customs and cultural identity, to ensure continued existence and to pass it on to their American-born children.

It is out of character for the Igbo to resettle permanently outside of Igboland. This may explain the immigrant Igbo penchant for nostalgic activities, activities that remind them of the land they left behind. The Igbo community in

108

Houston creates a world reminiscent to that found in their fatherland. Every Igbo is conscious of the fact that he/she belongs to a particular village and feels pride in belonging to that specific village; hence different villages organize themselves into groups, just as they are found in Igboland.

The Owerri Igbo organize themselves as the Greater Owerri Club (G. O. C.); those from the Old Bende Division call themselves the Old Bende Union of Texas. There are the Aros who organize themselves into the "Nzuko Umu Aro" (The congregation of the children of Aro). There are the Umuahia Group, the Ikwuano Sons and Daughters, the Ihitte Cultural Front, the Orlu Regional Assembly, the Isuikwuato Union, the Ndi Ichie Cultural Group, the Mbaise Group, the Mbaino, Obowo, Ngwa, Enugu, Awka, and on and on and on.

There are so far more than forty such groups in Houston, and others are yet to form their groups. Each of the states that make up Igboland also has a sub-central organization. For example, there is the Ndi Abia, USA in Houston, a group that caters to the needs of all Abia state indigenes in Houston, and whose goal is to carve and maintain a permanent link between the Igbo immigrants in Houston and their native land and exert significant influence in the governance of their state. The Anambra people also have such an organization, and so do the Enugu and the other states.

There is, however, a general organization, which serves as an umbrella for all the groups, and each subgroup belongs to this organization---The Igbo People's Congress. This organization caters to the needs and interests of all Igbo and sees to the preservation of Igbo culture and tradition.

This organization meets every third Wednesday of the month. This is arranged so as to make room for the meetings of the other groups, which usually take place on the first or last Sunday or Saturday of every month. It is important that all Igbo belong to their village group meetings and also the larger group. This is necessary in case of emergency.

However, the real unity on the tribal level lies in their consciousness to be Igbo. Their folk-tales, folk songs, riddles, proverbs, rituals, and festivals tell them about the glorious culture of their great ancestral land.

One important characteristic of the Igbo is that they are their brothers' keepers. There is no strict distinction made between distant relations or cousins, uncles, aunts, nephews, nieces, and so on. Everybody is *nwannem* (my brother or my sister). Also, as the Igbo say, *nwa bu nwa oha* (every child is everybody's child); hence they treat every child as they would their own. For an Igbo child, every adult Igbo male is "uncle" and every adult Igbo female is "auntie".

When a new child is born, the entire village gathers, singing, dancing, and rejoicing. Everyone contributes to the well-being of the mother and the new baby---bathing the baby, preparing food for the mother and the family, fetching water and firewood for cooking, sweeping the compound and the house, washing clothes and dishes, and so on---until the mother is strong enough to do things for and by herself. Here in Houston, despite tight schedules, they still find time to uphold this aspect of their culture. They make sure that each family experiences this ritual. This *omugwo,* as it is called, lasts for about six months.

Under normal circumstances, the Igbo do not leave the bodies of their dead to be buried in a foreign land. They must return to their fatherland to be buried. The organizations, both the close kin group and the umbrella organization, work closely together to make sure that the spirit of the dead is not left wandering in a far away land. They arrange for the transportation, funeral arrangements and the burial. This is made possible in part by the life insurance provided by the groups, which covers each registered member, by the generous donations from individual members, and by the funds from the organization's treasury.

During the period of this research, an illustrious son of Igbo was shot and killed. He was a professor in the School of Technology at Texas Southern University. Before the day was over, the news of his death had reached every Igbo. The telephone served as the traditional *ogene* (the Igbo town crier's metal gong) used to disseminate information across the land. Everyone was asked to assemble in the house of the dead man's uncle that night.

What transpired was similar to what Achebe (1959) recorded in *Things Fall Apart* when a daughter of Umuofia was killed. A town crier asked everyone to gather at the market place the next morning. Ogbuefi Ezeugo, furious and angry, told the people of Umuofia how their daughter was murdered by a neighboring clan. They sent out an ultimatum asking the clan to choose between war and the offer of a young virgin as compensation.

It was the same anger that rumbled silently within the crowd that gathered at this Southeast Houston home that gloomy night. There was a striking difference: The people of Umuofia were ready for revenge, for war, and they immediately dispatched both an ultimatum and an emissary of war. In this case, neither an ultimatum nor an emissary of war was dispatched. Discussions were tailored toward arrangements to take the body home. Their knowledge of the fact that there was nothing they could do in terms of revenge disempowered them and made that particular night more sinister and uncanny.

Although this Igbo did not attend his particular village group meetings, he was accorded all the respect due an Igbo; everyone contributed as much as (s)he could, believing, as the Igbo say, that when one celebrates another's funeral, (s)he is at the same time taking care of his/her own funeral. Their goal was not only to take the body home, but also to help make life easier for the deceased family of a wife and five children.

The importance of returning a body to be buried in Igboland cannot be overemphasized. The consequences of not doing so could be very disastrous. During one of the ceremonies observed during this research, one of the masquerades suddenly dashed into the audience in a rage, flinging its whip against tables, walls and even people. The women and some men in the area fled in silent confusion, but there was nowhere to run. Some people fell on each other, causing a huge stampede; some propped against the wall, squinting and sweating.

111

As soon as it made its way back to the dancing arena, someone threw a cold, raw egg on its face which splattered all over the place, even on people's clothes. The egg dripped down the mask like a weeping corsage. At that moment, the masquerade slowed down. Moments later, it left. It was the first masquerade to depart the arena.

The mask on the masquerade was dark-faced and seemed to express some qualities of "ugliness" and fierceness. It has two pierced eyes and gaping teeth. The pierced eyes seemed to express some inner agitation, some intrinsic unrest. This masquerade depicts a wandering ghost, the ghost of one of the Igbo who departed in a foreign land and has not reached its proper resting place. It was probably frustrated and began to vent its anger on the people. The symbolism of its appearance was to sensitize and remind the people of their responsibility.

It is not totally surprising that such a spirit possessed the masquerader because there are some Igbo who have died in Houston, but whose bodies, for some reason, did not make it home. It is this type of spirit that is placated during rituals so as to keep its aggression in check. It thus appears that the ancestral spirit and the mask form a single entity such that one cannot be dissociated from the other.

Most of the festivals, ceremonies and religious practices that the Igbo observe in Houston are done at the same time that they are observed in Igboland. One of the most important of these festivals is the New Yam festival, which brings together all the gods of the land, ancestors and all the people at one time and place to celebrate a fruitful harvest.

The Igbo understand the importance of this festival; hence, when they come, they adorn themselves in their original outfit---those that their ancestors recognize and identify with. These costumes communicate the same message. It takes no effort to sense in the wearers the glow of secure self-esteem. Although the elements of the costumes vary from person to person, the overall impression is one of beauty and grandeur, one of richness of culture and a positive sense of identity and pride.

112

The men's costumes varied considerably from the women's. The men adorned themselves in a complicated assemblage of garments. They appeared to exhibit a serene sense of self-assurance, which seemed to result from knowledge of their status as men combined with an awareness of the occasion. Some of the men wore caps on their heads which appeared to be made of leopard skin, some of brocade---green, red, white, blue and a combination of other colors.

There were others who wore hats, which appeared to be concocted of a variety of materials, ranging from leather to the most expensive of materials decorated with cowry shells, beads, and feathers. Some of the hats were sewn, stitched, plaited; others were woven, crocheted and appliquéd and elaborately embroidered.

Most of the men came with carved wooden staffs. Some of the staffs (or working sticks) had elephant heads carved on them; some had lion heads, while some were simply plain. Igbo men choose their staff to as a symbol of their position. A staff with an elephant head symbolizes strength; the lion symbolizes "The King of the Pride," and the tiger symbolizes agility and quickness.

A staff has always indicated a source of strength, something to lean on, and a guide. In the Bible, travelers used staff for support; shepherds used staff to guide the sheep, and Moses used staff to lead the children of Israel out of bondage. For the Igbo, staff also signifies authority, pride, strength, confidence, and power. Like the Psalmist wrote, "I will fear no evil; thy rod and thy staff, they comfort me."

Most of the staffs are made of wood, and wood holds a special place in Igbo culture. Igbo masks are made with wood, and the Iroko trees, from which the woods come, are believed to harbor the spirit of the departed.

Almost all the men wore strings of coral beads on their necks. Some of them wore more than one. Their garments were ankle-length, flowing with different motifs. These garments were worn over wide matching breeches and some over wraparounds that resembled the women's. The motifs on these garments were lion's head, tiger's head, dog's head, and elephant's head. These

113

garments and adornments reflect their oneness with nature. Most of the fabric was of silk, a natural object.

At all the festivals observed, there were specific men whose appearances drew the most attention. At one of these festivals, there was a man whose attire appeared distinctively different from the others. He wore a large loose robe of satin lace, richly trimmed and embroidered with intricate patterns of contrasting colors. He bunched this robe at the shoulders. His necklaces were strings of cowry shells and orange-colored, cylinder-like beads. His staff was of dazzling brass.

He also wore a crown-like hat made of a combination of gold and red velvet. He was also holding a leather fan edged with ostrich plumes and a whisk which looked more like the tail of a horse. His footwear was a pair of highly designed sandals. All the men he met on his way greeted him in a very special way -- beating their fans against his three times to the side and then concluding with a stroke at the middle. Those that were not holding fans simulated with their bare hands. He was the Chief Ritualist.

The Chief Ritualist serves as the Chief Priest, a Reverend Father in the Christian religion who performs Mass or the sacrament of Holy Communion. He is believed to be in close proximity with the spiritual forces, knows how to tap the vital energy, and, therefore, serves as the intercessor between the spirits and the people, a bridge between two worlds---the mortal world and the spiritual world.

He receives the messages of the higher order, in silence, just like the biblical prophets of the Old Testament. He knows when the time is right to eat, when the gods have given their okay, and he communicates the same to his people.

He is a traditional father who sits at the head of the table and commands the respect of all, and because of his position, he wields strong traditional power. This power stems in part from the people's tacit awareness of the existence of spirits and the world beyond, their religious inclination and their knowledge of the Supernatural. This power is cultural; hence internal to the people's volition.

114

There is consent on the part of the audience, cringing humility based on their knowledge and acceptance of the norm, the culture, the tradition. This power becomes more manifest given the understanding that, under normal circumstances, the Igbo pays no allegiance to any ruler or central authority. During one of the ceremonies, the people were very hungry, but they would not eat until he had asked them to do so.

The women came in what appeared to be their traditional wraparound fashion, each of which appeared to portray certain knowledge of each individual's taste. The wraparounds were long draped cloths, which extend from the waist to the heels. Most of the women were rather loaded than adorned with gold necklaces, pendants and bracelets.

One could not help but hear the rustling of clothes and the ringing, chiming and clanking of accumulation of metal bangles. They were dressed in Gold, Satin, and Organza laces with colors of taupe, vibrant reds, radiant greens, and banana yellows. Their headdress was exceedingly flamboyant and flared as they gathered at the top of the head like fans, twisted on the side of the head like a newly opened rose petal.

The children's outfits were not as sophisticated and complicated as those of the adults. The boys wore the traditional sleeveless tunics, trousers and hats, some of which matched and some of which did not match. Some of the little girls were dressed in wraparounds, blouses, and head-ties. Some of them wore leotards underneath their dancing gears. Some parents adorned their children just like themselves.

Everyone came in anticipation of the appearance of the visitors from the underworld to unite with the living. They came ready to be reassured and entertained. They waited patiently.

One thing is sure: Distance and the pressure of acculturation have not completely barred the appearance of the spirits from the underworld. When the masks and masquerades do appear, they do so as authentically and as genuinely as they appear in Igboland.

One of the most important aspects of these ceremonies, at least as far as this study is concerned and as Achebe (1984) notes, is that Igbo masquerades have provided a major stimulus for the arts---sculpture, music, singing, dancing, drama and even architecture. In fact, as we shall see, and as Jefferson (19730 also points out, "the artist's contribution to the ceremonies is often as great as that of the individual performer" (p. 64).

CHAPTER 8

Masking Traditions

Ladd (1973) points out that every culture has nodal points, points at which important strands of a culture seem to intersect, and as a consequence, serve as focal points for understanding the culture. African art serves such purpose. Among the Igbo, for instance, mask carving serves as a nodal point. It draws together all aspects of Igbo culture, which includes but is not limited to masquerade, religious rituals, and initiation.

Igbo society is characterized by democracy, religious sanctions, individualism, and the glorification of personal success. They create a remarkable art, which is almost entirely religious in purpose. Due to the diversity of the Igbo people, it will not be possible to generalize about a pure Igbo art style. Since every Igbo community carves and uses masks, this study concentrated mainly on mask carving among the Igbo.

Mask carving among the Igbo is the most important aspect of their art. It portrays vividly their belief in ancestral power and the existence of spirits. Through mask carving, they communicate with the dead fathers of the clan through whom they receive protection, power, and fertility. It serves as a strong magnetic force that binds them together and provides the desired unity and stability of the tribe. Its role is to reaffirm, at regular intervals, the truth and the immediate presence of myths in everyday life.

Like other African masks, Igbo mask strengthens the collective existence of the whole tribe in all its complex aspects and, as Laude (1971) adds, "recalls noteworthy events of an early period which structured the world and the society" (p.140). The mask serves as the medium through which the Igbo converse with the ancestors and solicit them with the most varied requests.

At harvest time and during New Yam festivals, the spirits of the ancestors are invoked in order to honor them and give them thanks. During planting season, before the crops are sowed, the aid and protection of the ancestors are solicited in order to ensure fecundity, to send rain in times of severe drought. During judicial proceedings, they are called to pass divine judgment.

Igbo masks, like other African masks, represent, as Bravemann (1974) states, the active dynamic aspects by furnishing the means by which the pressing problems of existence can be comprehended and resolved. Leuzinger (1960) also adds that the active intervention of the masks are solicited when a man feels himself threatened by demons against whom he can do nothing with his natural resources.

Because the Igbo, like other African tribes, believe in the ancestors as the source of life and prosperity, and a fixed point of reference, they see the ancestors as strong and powerful. Therefore, in creating the mask, the artist, motivated primarily by ritual purpose, tries not to portray an individual. He knows that he is reproducing collective tribal conception of a four-dimensional being--- one that does not resemble any known human being.

The Igbo artist does not work to create realism. The part of the figure he chisels out of wood is not the part of any recognizable body. It is this divine detachment that causes the Igbo ancestral figure to resemble nothing known to mankind.

Umezinwa (1980) notes that the actions of the artist consist of a conscious and unconscious geometrical exploration of space, stating, "this exploration ends up by being a singular discovery that signifies what it does not resemble" (p. 14). He describes the final outcome of this unique artistic expression as "an artistic miracle".

The Igbo artist is, therefore, not as concerned with pleasing the human eye as he is with satisfying the spirit. For this reason, even though a god is conceived

118

in the image of a man, it must not have any resemblance to any particular individual. Through conscious distortion of proportions, the artist expresses a neutral image, achieving the idea of an ancestor. This justifies the profuse use of stylization in faces and any other forms that could bear resemblance to any known human forms.

Some have argued that African artists distort proportions because they lack the "artistic" skill to render objects naturalistically. This is not true. These artists are capable of representing anything as it is. However, their main concern is to create a larger than life image; hence they consciously distort proportions to achieve this inner reality.

Someone who does not understand Picasso's work would think, looking at his Cubistic portraits, that he lacked the "artistic" skill to render humans naturalistically. The world knows that this is untrue. The religious artists of the Renaissance portrayed the Virgin Mary and the Christian Saints as purely and perfectly as they could, with smooth, healthy skins and bodies, with halos and even with hearts of gold. It was an attempt to represent spirits, to detach them from ordinary human beings.

The same could be found even in other religions. The supernatural power of the Indian god of destruction, Shiva, is expressed by the multiplicity of its hands, while the mystery of Buddha is portrayed in its silent and mystical repose. It is the same concept that finds expression in the art of the Igbo---the internal strength and energy represented by the closed eyes of some Igbo masks and the restful postures of their carved figures.

Mask carving among the Igbo is a serious matter; it takes time, patience and skill. A good carver does not take his work lightly. He is just as committed to his work as were the religious painters of the Renaissance era. He knows, as Bodrogi (1968) points out, that the erection of an ancestral cult object is a supremely sacred act, and that the essence of the mask, which he is about to create, is to establish relationship with the supernatural powers.

This is one reason why the carver initially has to acquire a wide range of imagination, which will relate to the forms he wants to depict. Again, he has to imagine himself as one of the masks. By so doing, he is able to ascertain the dramatic behaviors associated with the masks; hence he is able to lay emphasis where necessary. This way, the forms, which his work expresses, reflect the mood such as anger, fierceness, and other emotions relating to various fundamental beliefs of the people.

The most important masks are carved by the medicine man. He is said to be the interpreter of the people's minds. Other independent artists could also carve the masks. To be a good mask carver, the artist must be initiated into the masquerade society, like the *ekpe* or the *okonko*. He must have been purified through the rites of the cult, must be inspired by the exalted religious function of his work, and, as Rodrigues (1974) also adds, must be spiritually prepared to perform his art such that the finished work will portray his virtuosity, his imagination and his sensitivity.

Different Igbo communities have different names for the masquerade society. In Otampa, it is called *enyi mara enyi amaghi* (A friend, the initiated, knows what his friend, the uninitiated, does not know). This name points to the all-important oath binding the members. It instills into the members a sense of responsibility, of trust and of discipline.

No matter how close the initiate's relationship is to the uninitiated, he must not reveal the secrets of the masquerade society. In Umuokogbue, another Igbo community in Isuikwuato, the masquerade is called *okonko* (the ominous). Among the Bende community, it is called *mboko* (the awesome).

These secret societies play an important role in Igbo art. They act in the name of the ancestors and the spirits who created them and who are embodied in the masks. They are made up of people believed to have common link or who are nearest in contact with the spirit world. They are those who want to reach out to the source of all life through the mask agency, and they assume that the ancestors support their activities. They regard themselves as superhuman and therefore tend to be highly organized.

Because they are sure of themselves and sure of the powers they receive from above and below, they assume the responsibility of making peace and controlling the people. They maintain order and settle disputes. To become a member of the secret society, one has to be a man of tested discipline.

The masks serve as executive agents, and they punish every breach of custom. They represent police and legal authority. Wherever there is danger and lurking of evil sorcerers who cannot be dealt with by material means, the masks are brought to play. Such masks are generally referred to as the guardian spirit masks.

During funerals and when the souls of the dead are driven out so that they may set out on their journey to *ala ndi nmuo* (the land of the dead), masks like the *Agbogho nmuo* (the maiden spirit mask) and the *Okiti* masquerade are called to play. Such masks, observes Herold (1967), "embody the spirit of the deceased who, through the mask, can speak, for the last time, to his people" (p. 85).

Achebe (1959) records the appearance of such masks at the funeral of an old man, Ogbuefi Ezeudu, a great man. Because he was great, almost everyone was present at his funeral. It was a warrior's funeral. Amid the beating of the ancient drums of death, the firing of canons, and men dashing about in frenzy, cutting down trees and animals in their way, the ancestral spirit appeared from the underworld, speaking in an esoteric voice.

Although religious function is here linked to social function, it was due to the secret society that the making of masks had developed. Whenever a quarrel in a society defies human settlement, it is the secret society, through its agency, the masquerade, which gives the final verdict.

The appearance of the spirits from the underworld on occasions like this is worth noting. A good example is in Achebe's *Things Fall Apart* when *egwugwu* (the incarnated spirits) emanated from the spirit world and settled a deep and long-lasting quarrel with a single dispatch. As the iron gong sounded, the people waited to behold the departed fathers of the land. When they finally appeared, the awe of their appearance sent shock waves through the spines of those involved in the dispute. In matter of minutes, the dispute was settled.

The Ritual of Sanctity

The creative process of the mask itself is a complex ritual. Because the making of an ancestral cult object is a sacred act, and aware that he is creating an abode for the spirit -- an emanation of god-- the artist sets about his task with great devotion and concentration. He makes very careful preparations, which include fasting, purification, and abstention from any form of contact with women. Then he withdraws into the seclusion of the bush where he begins his work in silence. This enables him to devote himself to his work with perfect sanctity.

Under this condition, the artist is inspired by a vision, a dream, and he feels within himself the will to create. Duerden (1971) notes:

> *Any element in man that strives after change, invention and creativity uses the power of the earth, of the forest and of the bush, which is constantly remaking and re-forming itself (p. 67).*

This could explain why the Igbo artist chooses the bush, the forest as a place for solitude; why John the Baptist and Jesus Christ Himself sought solitude in the wilderness; why the burning bush was the chosen place for Moses to receive the mandate from God to set His people free, and why Elijah secluded himself in the Brook.

The Ritual of Propitiation

Before cutting the wood and before beginning to carve, the artist performs a series of sacrifices and rituals to avoid becoming a victim of the spirit, which he summons by this activity and to avoid being injured by the tools. The spirit

122

already dwelling in the tree that will be felled must be propitiated. Disturbance allowance must be paid. The cutting down of a tree is not merely a technical action; the tree contains forces, which will not be dispossessed without a struggle. It contains its own force, like all living things, and often that of a spirit, which has chosen it as a habitat. The artist is aware that he is ejecting a spirit from its abode and rendering it homeless, that he is setting a dangerous force in motion.

Having been so ejected, the spirit wanders malevolently in search of whom to vent its anger on. A sacrifice is offered to call on a more powerful spirit to keep this wandering spirit in check. Moreover, because the forest is the home of powers worshipped by a definite cult, it is important to compensate them for the tree, which is about to be removed.

During the carving process, the artist becomes encaged by the influence of the spirit, which he is trying to represent. The visible and the invisible world, the human and the divine, the past and the present, all form one harmonious whole, and the artist has to fit himself into this unity. During this time, taboos must not be violated, rites of passage and other rituals must be observed, and spirits must be appeased.

The works are carved neither to interest a human audience nor as representations of spirits, but as objects within which the spirit may dwell. The artist does not seek to create a portrait, but to catch the inner quality of what is portrayed.

The Ritual of Invitation

After the carving is completed, a priest invokes the right spirit in the finished work. With rattles, bells, and chants, the spirit is invited to take its place in the image. If it favors the figure with its presence, then the figure becomes imbued with its power, which is automatically transmitted to those present at the ceremony.

Sacrifices of different kinds enhance its vitality. It is presented with kolanuts and freshly tapped palm-wine. The souls of the departed sip the

123

sacrificial blood poured over the mask. During harvest, the first fruits are offered to the ancestral mask. After a successful hunting expedition, a share of the animal caught is also offered.

OJI: Oke Osisi

Igbo masks are carved mostly with wood. The wood used for mask carving possesses some power, a vital energy, a life force, a force that is anything but remote, a force whose presence is constantly present and continuously in operation, a force which, as Schmalenbach (1988) notes, "lives in closest proximity to the people, in a nearby tree, in a rocky outcrop, in streams, in the souls of the dead, and often in the wood figures carved for them" (p. 14).

The artist respects the characteristics of the wood and tries not to diminish the power of this working force in the carving process. As Umezinwa (1980) notes, what one finds as a result is the metamorphosis of wood into pure mystical emotion. It is this mystical emotion that attracts the ancestral spirit to the mask and creates a real psychic connection between the carved mask and the ancestral spirit. This unique characteristic of the Igbo mask, says Vevers (1974), renders it "devoid of any vitiating imitation" (p. 30).

Some of the most frequently used wood are *Oji* and *Ogirisi* (mahogany species) because of their durability and sanctity. The *Oji* (Iroko) particularly is believed to have male and female types, which are distinguished from each other by their impotency and fertility respectively. The male *Iroko* stands tall with little or no branches, and bats do not reside in it (nocturnal winged mammals associated with spirits). The female iroko, on the other hand, has lots of branches and fruits. It is believed to be the abode of spirits, and bats live in it.

In Igbo philosophy, *Oji* is recognized as the king of trees, a position it earned in the spirit world. Undecided spirits, spirits that have not made up their minds what to become during reincarnation, reside in the *Oji* until such a time that they have decided. Such spirits are neither in the spirit world nor in the world of

124

the living. These are the spirits that are ejected and checked before the tree is felled.

People are named after this tree, and those so named are often called *Oke Osisi* (the Great Tree). For the Igbo, *Oji* is a part of existence, and it is therefore the most suitable for transporting the life force of a spirit or an ancestor. It is said in Igbo that "there is Oji in every compound." In other words, there is always one great person in every family.

All Igbo masks have little or no effect without costumes. Although some African wood sculptures stand still and convey their interior energy by a sense of arrested movement (Davidson, 1971), Igbo masks, seen as the visible expression of the invisible, are intended to be seen in movement, in a dance, and in full costume. Therefore, in order to appreciate a carved mask, one needs to see it in movement, possibly, above eye level.

Moreover, to isolate a mask (as it is frequently done in museums) is to take out its meaningful context. The mask itself is regarded as a part of a complex structure, a part of a costume, which is danced into music. It is only when all these elements are present that the mask comes to life and becomes inhabited by the spirit.

In Achebe's *Things Fall Apart,* Edogo, the carver expressed dissatisfaction after completing a commissioned mask. Although the owners praised the mask very highly, Edogo still felt disappointed. He knew, however, that he must see the mask in action, in movement, in motion, in a dance, in order to determine its quality, accuracy, and efficacy.

The Ritual of Invocation

Before he wears the mask, the mask dancer must undergo special prohibitions and make special sacrifices. Just like the artist (the mask carver), the actor (the mask dancer) observes prohibitions, mainly of sexual nature. This he must do in order to protect himself from death or from being possessed by evil

125

spirits during the time of performance. Then he goes into the shrine for the invocation ritual.

This ritual must be performed before the mask dancer wears the mask. It invokes the gods, the spirits, and the ancestors into the land to dwell among the people. Only the initiates in the masquerade society participate in this ritual.

The mask is placed on the altar, and the chief priest, usually the oldest of the initiates, begins to speak in an esoteric tongue---an incantation which invokes the spirits. He pours libation of palm-wine on the ground and asks the spirits to emanate with all their blessings for the community. He breaks kolanut and throws some pieces on the ground, chews some and spits them on the mask.

Then he begins to speak again in a guttural voice, swaying, gyrating, and responding to the voices of the unknown, the voices of a higher order. At this point, he picks up the mask and places it on the head of the mask dancer who is now completely attired in the costume of the masquerade.

As soon as the mask sits perfectly on his face, he is no longer the simple villager. The ritual is complete, and now the masquerade---the mask and the costumed mask dancer---is ready to enter the arena. The other initiates accompany him to the village ground where the performance is to take place. Gunshots, ovation, stampede, and roar herald its appearance.

In order to get a spirit to manifest itself through the masquerade, a great deal of effort is required by the dancer who wears the mask. The atmosphere is raised to fever pitch. The drums beat, the flutes sing, and chants pierce the still tight air. Spellbound by the intensity of his belief, the wearer of the mask feels himself permeated and transformed by its power.

Soon, he falls into a state of ecstasy and begins to act the part of the spirit he is evoking. He speaks with a change in his voice, and performs with strange steps the movements by which the spirit is exorcised. At that moment, he is the master; his commands are obeyed without question and his requests granted without undue hesitation.

It is important to note that all Igbo masks are considered spirits. Even those that are said to be 'weak' possess a certain aura and mystique (Cole and Aniakor, 1984).

The appearance of a mask is breathtaking. The wearer of the mask believes that the gods are manifesting themselves through him. When possessed, he could dance for hours without stopping. Bravmann's (1974) describes it succinctly:

> The appearance of the mask is the invisible manifestation of a god. The dwelling place is not only the object of wood, but also the man it envelops; the spirit takes possession of both of them. So long as the divine presence lasts, the mask (the wearer and the thing worn) belongs to the world of the sacred. As soon as the spirit takes possession, the wearer finds himself in a pathological state of trance, and he is, therefore, no longer himself. It is the god who now acts through him (p. 31).

Certain sculptural qualities make some masks too harsh for the human gaze. The entire masquerade is directed toward the spirit, not toward the spectator. A mask may evoke revulsion, for example, *njokaoya* masquerade (ugliness worse than disease). A man's ugliness is usually compared to a spirit mask. Moreover, pregnant women are advised not to look at masks, lest their children acquire its big eyes and long nose, and therefore turn out ugly.

The power of the mask to influence the ancestors depends on the social prestige of the owner, since a man can only reach prominence with their help, and his success shows that the ancestors favor him. An inherited mask retains its power over the ancestors, and the more prestigious its owner was in this life, the more powerful he will be as an ancestor. It is not the case that every dead Igbo becomes an ancestor, just as it is not true that every dead Christian becomes a Saint.

Ancestorship is a rank that must be attained. First of all, one must attain old age; hence those who die young suffer dual frustration both in the world of the living and in the spirit world. They remain boys in both worlds (Uchendu, 1965).

Old age is a necessary but not sufficient attribute of a would-be ancestor. One must have been a strong, hardworking man, trustworthy, and honest, one who commands the respect of all his people. In *Things Fall Apart,* although Unoka, Okonkwo's father, was old, he lacked the qualities of a would-be ancestor.

He was a lazy man and left no inheritance for his son. He owed almost every man he knew, and his death was a miserable one. He died of a swollen stomach, which was an abomination to *Ala,* the earth goddess.

When a man dies of such a disease, he is not buried in the ground; he is carried to the Evil Forest and left to die. Such a man could not be honored as an ancestor. Even his own children would not. An account in Achebe's (1959) *Things Fall Apart* of a man who consulted an oracle to find a solution to a pressing problem echoes this sentiment:

> ...*The Oracle said, "Your dead father wants you to sacrifice a goat to him. "Do you know what he told the Oracle? He said, "Ask my dead father if he ever had a fowl when he was alive" (p.23).*

The difference between Igbo ancestors and the other deities is that the ancestors are of the living persons' kin while the deities are distinctly removed from them. The ancestors are closer to the deities than are the living; hence they serve as the intercessors.

Old masks, which span several generations, are considered especially powerful. Some authors say that masks that are old and chipped are discarded, but they fail to specify why this is so. It is important to point out here that old masks are discarded, not simply because they are old, but because the process of creation is valued more among the Igbo than the finished product. There is a reason for this, and Achebe (1984) expresses it very eloquently:

The Igbo choose to eliminate the product and retain the process so that every occasion and every generation will receive its own impulse and experience of creation (p. ix).

Different masks are assigned different duties. The peace preserving masks are usually ritualistic in character and masculine in vigor. By the force of their physical forms, they brutalize the onlooker. Such masks have mysterious, tortured and often terrifying lines which, according to Davidson, 1971), express the ultimate in supernatural forces. Their forms are most expressive, most inspiring, and utterly impregnable.

Some of the best masks are designed with awesome as well as sensational motifs. Some of these motifs include snakes, contorted faces suffering from terrible disease and deformities, or furious animal forms, for example, the tiger and its gaping teeth. In addition, the materials used in creating these masks could transmit horror. Example of such materials include skins and skulls of slaughtered enemies, libations showing dark spots of blood and yokes of eggs that were smeared on the mask for quite a good number of years.

Summary

To really understand the Igbo mask, one must observe it as a dynamic element of a complicated dramatic ensemble in the intricate rhythm of the ritual. To regard the mask merely as wooden face carving or as a helmet would be ridiculous; to consider it static, hung on the wall, or placed on a pedestal would be sheer betrayal and deceit.

The Igbo mask is not just a disguise that the wearer uses to hide his identity; it is not a man pretending to be a god, but a god who becomes visible in its flesh and blood, in its real form. Herold (1967) notes that when wearing his mask, the Igbo man "does not represent a supernatural being. In the eyes of his fellow tribesmen, the supernatural being really exists and becomes embodied in the mask throughout the time of its appearance" (p. 85).

The mask is inviolable. This is why the artist who creates the mask does not try to imitate a human face but aims at bringing to life the most expressive part of the ephemeral body of a force more powerful than man.

A closer look at the masks of the Igbo reveals that almost all of them are heads. No other part of the body is carved, although they are covered with costumes. This characteristic goes to portray the Igbo belief that the head is the seat of the life force (Davidson, 1971) or the seat of intellectual powers (Leuzinger, 1960; Balandier and Maquet, 1974).

It is a taboo, by Igbo tradition, for women to see or touch certain masks. Unfortunately, when these masks began to be displayed under the powerful lighting of museums, they become exposed to women. This single act, says Rachewiltz (1966) deprives the Igbo of their traditional, spiritual, and cultural patrimony.

It is encouraging to note that the masks and ancestral wooden figures such as found in the museums are ancestral figures in isolation. Umezinwa (1980) describes them as passive art objects and ineffective symbols of distant spirits that cannot be compared to the active ancestral figures and masks employed during religious worship around which hovers an invoked ancestral spirit capable of protecting or punishing a community.

CHAPTER 9

Your God, Our God

The art of Africa can be viewed from different perspectives. As a means of communication with the supernatural being, African art has a religious function. As an eloquence of the inarticulate, its silence speaks louder than words, and this silence explodes into a rhythmic sensation during performance.

The following three chapters will examine these perspectives in detail. For purposes of efficacy and clarity, the art of the Igbo will be used as a point of contact in examining these perspectives.

Religion and the Art of the Igbo

To understand the art of the Igbo, as with most non-Western cultures, one must have a genuine knowledge of their religious beliefs and practices (Srozenski, 1991). For the Igbo, as for other African tribes, religion and art are so deeply intertwined that it is difficult to speak of one without the other, and they express their deepest values and longings. The Igbo worldview has been primarily religious. They believe that each individual has a destiny, *chi*, and that this destiny is ascribed in the palm of the person's hand as *akara aka*. It is this *akara aka,* which is believed to lead the person through life (*akara aka onye n'edu ya*).

Thus if, for example, one dies a sudden death, people say that it was the person's decision with his *chi* (*O bu ka ya na Chi ya kpebiri*). Conversely, if a person prospers and leads a good life, people say that his God is good (*Chi ya di mma*) or that he is lucky (*O bu onye Chi oma*).

131

Predestination

The Igbo believe in God as the Almighty; hence they give names such as *Chika* (God is Supreme), *Kelechi* (give thanks to God), *Chijindu* (God, the author of life), *Chinenyenwa* (God, the giver of children), *Chidimma* (God is good), *Chizuruoke* (God is perfect), *Chinedu* (God leads), *Chukwuemeka* (God has done well). The word "*Chi*" could mean luck, destiny, or God, depending on the context in which it is used.

A person's destiny is decided in the beginning of the person's life. Duerden (1971) notes that the individuals select their length of life and their future life activities at the point they choose to enter the world. Those individuals could not rise beyond the destiny of their chi (Achebe, 1959). It is at the point of reincarnation that such decisions are made.

For the Igbo, reincarnation is not only the bridge between the living and the dead, but also a necessary precondition for the transaction and transfer of social status from the world of humanity to the world of the dead (Uchendu, 1965). It is at reincarnation that individuals work out proper roles for themselves through face-to-face interaction with the Creator.

Just as Plato, the philosopher, would agree, it is the reincarnated soul that determines the person's class in the society. It is not expected that everyone make the right choice in the beginning of life; however, a wrong choice does not automatically spell doom for the individual. It is here that Igbo art comes to play. With sacrifices and invocations, people may better their luck in this life or during the next life.

The *Ikenga*

The Igbo use works of art, for example, *Ikenga* (personal god or the strength of a man's right hand) to ascertain that the decision made earlier remains or to solicit the help of the ancestors in making sure that the person's hands remain clean (*na aka ya di ocha*). The *Ikenga* represents "the existential soul which is supposed to be seated in the right hand and forearm and which an individual cultivates in his search for self-definition" (Duerden, 1971, p. 66).

The Ikenga exemplifies the ability of the owner to deal with life and fortunes. Also, one may change his destiny by appealing to the gods through a priest who performs some rituals to the *Ikenga* or any other god designated.

The Supreme Being

The Igbo also believe in a Supreme Being --- *Chi Ukwu* (the Great God) --- that has been contracted to *Chukwu* or *Chineke* (the God who creates), the Creator of heaven and earth. Some have translated "*Chi-na-eke*" as God and Creation (Cole and Aniakor, 1984). In some parts of Igboland, the Supreme Being is addressed during sacrifices as *Abassi di n'elu*.

This name is derived from a combination of Igbo and Ibibio languages. "*Abassi*" translates "God" in Ibibio language while the suffix "*di n'elu*" translates "in heaven" in Igbo. Put together, "*Abassi di n'elu*" translates "God who dwells in heaven". Other names for God in Igbo include "*Chukwu Abiama*" and "*Olisa*".

The Duity

The Igbo perceive this God as directly unapproachable; hence they devised a means of reaching Him. An immigrant articulates this concept very well. He explains that *Chukwu* is the Godhead, a culmination of the Igbo philosophy of the Duity, *Chi na Eke*, a two-in-one God, which has been contracted to *Chineke*. *Chi* is God the Father; *Eke* is God the Destiny, which, like the spirit, is in everyone and controls one's action on earth.

The difference between the Christian belief in the Trinity and the Igbo belief in the Duity is the idea of the son---God the Son. In Igbo religion, God is conceived as a High Spirit, which cannot be associated with a son. The logic here is that if He has a son, then He must have a wife, a human characteristic, and that will distort His high spiritual image as far as the Igbo is concerned.

133

Uchendu's (1965) describes the Igbo high Gods a withdrawn God who has finished his work on earth and watches over His children from a distance. He is a satisfied god who is not jealous of prosperity of man on earth (p. 96).

Uchendu's description could be alluded to in Hebrew religion, during the time of Moses. Because their God was invisible, the Israelites asked Aaron to make for them a god that they could see. It is an attempt to make allowance for the weakness of mankind that brings art to play in Igbo religion---art, which gives a visualizing, tangible effect. It is the same human weakness that causes other religions to erect images in the temples, images that give them the opportunity to fixate their faith, to utilize the services of the visible in the service of the invisible.

An Igbo who sacrifices and prays before a carved wooden figure is not worshipping the figure; just as a Christian who kneels and prays before a carved image or statue of the Virgin Mary is not necessarily worshipping the Virgin. Another immigrant expressed his views thus:

We don't worship idols. We worship God. We believe in God. Was it the White man that gave us the name? God is God. He is God. What about the Creator: What about Olisa? We have so many names for God, so many names. The Igbo believe strongly in God. The White man came and did not understand what we were talking about. They came and concluded that we are idol worshippers. They did not understand at all. The God we worship is not the one the White man understands. It was when the White man came that we knew that there was someone called Jesus. We were able to recognize the White man's holy people, but they refused to recognize our own holy people and called them idols. There is no difference between our carved statues and those that the White men keep in their churches, for example, the cross and the Virgin Mary and so on. There is no difference at all. The only difference is that the White man came and defeated us. You see, and then we became Bushmen. Then everything of ours became condemned. If you go now into a Catholic altar or Protestant altar and break their statue into pieces, people will scream, and scream and scream. Everyone will say that you have desecrated the land; you have committed an abomination; you have done this and that. Think of it. I am not saying that it is good. That thing is a statue; it is not Jesus, and it is not Mary. It is a symbol. All these things are representations. You cannot go and break them, or throw them away because it will be a desecration. It will then become a sacrilege. Why? Because they understood ours as idols, and we are idol worshippers. We are not worshipping idols at all.

In order words, the Igbo do not perceive these carved objects as idols. They are much more than that. In fact, a carved object is regarded as sacred only when a spirit inhabits it. The objects are symbolic representations imbued with metaphorical meaning (Umezinwa (1980).

The Mystical Medium

Relationships exist between a carved wooden figure or mask and an ancestral spirit. Umezinwa (1980) describes these relationships as the inclusion and exclusion relationships. In the inclusion relationship, the ancestral spirit and the wooden figure or mask form a single entity such that one cannot be dissociated from the other.

The worshipper does not attach the same degree of importance to the wooden figure or mask as he does to the ancestral spirit. To the worshipper, the figure or mask is a mystical medium of a dominant component---the ancestral spirit---for as long as the spirit resides in it.

On the other hand, when a spirit escapes from the figure or the mask---like the ones in the museums---, the relationship becomes that of eternal exclusion. Umezinwa clarifies this further with an example in Achebe's *Arrow of God* when the angry people of Aninta burnt their deity, *Ogba,* because it killed them instead of their enemies.

That signifies that it was not the invisible deity that was burned and destroyed, but the wooden figure, the mystical medium. The spirit escaped the figure during destruction, but thereafter, that spirit will no longer have a place to live from where it can kill or save people.

135

"Just a Piece of Wood"

An account in Achebe's (1959) *Things Fall Apart* helps clarify the Igbo concept of God and their belief system. This conversation was between Mr. Brown, the white missionary who visited Umuofia, an Igbo village, to convert them to Christianity and Akunna, one of the great men of the village. In this dialogue, Akunna explained to Mr. Brown that he believed in God:

> *"We also believe in Him and call Him Chukwu. He made all the world and the other gods."*
> *"There are no other gods," said Mr. Brown. "Chukwu is the only God and all others are false. You carve a piece of wood --- like that one"* (he pointed at the rafters from which Akunna's carved Ikenga hung), *"and you call it a god. But it is still a piece of wood."*
> *"Yes," said Akunna. "It is indeed a piece of wood. Chukwu made the tree from which it came.*
> *(pp. 164 - 165).*

Akunna's religion is not far removed from Mr. Brown's. At least, each one of them believes in one Supreme Being. In addition, each of them worshipped Him through intermediaries. Akunna would insist that the ancestors are equivalent to the Christian "saints", the dead who intercede for their children. Just as the Christian church in the 19th Century set aside November 1 to honor all its saints (Borten, 1965), so also do the Igbo celebrate harvest and New Yam to honor their own saints---their ancestors.

"Helps to Devotion"

Umezinwa (1980) observes that although most modern Protestant churches no longer use images, Catholics still do. According to him, the Catholics regard images of Christ and the Virgin Mary as "Helps to devotion" (p.19). It is this same concept that Akunna is attempting to explain to Mr. Brown. The Igbo ancestral masks and figures are equally "Helps to devotion". For the

Igbo, however, this Supreme Being, this High God, is the Energy that differentiates life from matter; He is the Life-force (Davidson, 1971).

Amadioha : **The god of thunder**

Very important for ritual in Igbo is the spirit of storm. This storm deity is known as *Amadioha Ezeigwe* (the owner of the skies). Amadioha lives in the sun and manifests itself in lightning and in thunder. The priest of the storm deity has the power to make rain fall and also to make rain cease. This priest is a wise man who observes the signs of the times and the secrets of nature. He is a prophet, like Elijah in the Old Testament of the Bible, who can tell whether small clouds in the distance will bring rain. Throughout the time of his services, he will neither take a bath nor drink water.

Ala: **The Earth Mother**

Belief in a spiritual power animating the earth is almost universal, but it is held very highly among the Igbo. The Earth is thought of as a female. She has a mystical power of which everybody stands in awe because of its prohibitions and punishments. Because she has been there since the beginning of the universe, she has gained the status of a spirit. Everyone must pass through her between death and reincarnation. She is therefore always in constant communion with this whole passage between life forms. She is responsible for recycling life both in the plant and in the animal world, the overseer of all supreme reproductions.

Ala is a merciful mother who intercedes for her children. Other minor deities may not take action against an Igbo without first bringing their complaints to *Ala*, but no spirit intervenes when *Ala* decides to punish. She is the ultimate judge of morality and conduct, does not punish in haste, and does not kill for minor offenses. She kills for offenses such as incest and murder.

Ala increases the fertility and the productivity of the land. Without her, life would be difficult for the Igbo who attach much sentiment to the land on whom their means of livelihood depend.

Spirits are solicited during planting season. In the spring, farmers offer sacrifices of fowl to *Ala* before tilling the soil, praying for permission to dig, for protection against accidents, and for a fruitful harvest. If one has problem with fecundity, he would go to the shrine of *Ala* to find out why. There is an account in Achebe's (1959) *Things Fall Apart* when Unoka, the farmer, went to visit Chika, the priestess of Agbala, to find out why he always had an unfruitful harvest. As he began to explain, the priestess stopped him and said:

> *Hold your peace! You have offended neither the gods nor your fathers. And when a man is at peace with his gods and his ancestors, his harvest will be good or bad according to the strength of his arm. You, Unoka, are known in all the clan for the weakness of your machete and your hoe.... Go home and work like a man" (p. 20).*

The earth is also concerned with the dead, and before a grave is dug, a libation is poured and permission asked. After harvest, before the new yam is eaten, it is first presented to *Ifejioku*, the god of yams, and *Ala*, the goddess of the land or Mother Earth. As a mother, the Earth gives fertility to crops, and also to human beings; as the queen of the underworld, she receives the dead into her womb (Achebe, 1984).

In summary, it is evident that religion empowers the Igbo artist and provides for him a source of inspiration. It is to appease the gods, to tap the powers of the supernatural, and to gain control of their environment that mask carving among the Igbo originated. The art, however, is not the object of worship, but it serves as the dwelling place of a spirit, as a means of communication, as "helps to devotion."

CHAPTER 10

Silence and the Art of the Igbo

*"If you do not understand my silence, you
will not understand my words."*
--- D. Tannen and M. Saville-Troike

The above statement articulates powerfully the role of silence in the art of
the Igbo. To really understand their art, one must understand their silence.

The theme of silence is a universal phenomenon, expressed in different
ways by different artists all through the ages. The symbolist artists of the 19th
century, for example, utilized silent images as a symbolist expression.

In his painting, "The Pieta", 1980, Emily Bernard positioned the people
standing silently over the body of the dead Christ laid beside a skull and bones
and set before a backdrop of a mystical landscape. The painting expresses an
inner mystery of human existence and vitiates the congruence between form and
idea, between the seen and unseen, the living and the dead. As Auchard (1986)
notes, such silence provides a delicately balanced emblem of man's existential
ambiguities.

Silence could evoke images that are as comfortable as a shawl thrown
around one's shoulders. It could also create a vacuum in which one could not
breathe. It could be a lack of everything, a foretaste of the tomb. It could be
distressing and misery-laden, consoling and peace bearing.

The images which silence creates could appear odd, curious, and strange,
articulating the unspeakable. Silence is a distinct tendency toward the inwardness
of the mystic, involving rejection of the word as inappropriate expression of a
purely inner and spiritual experience. It is the original stillness of the cosmos, the
unspeakable mystery of the divine.

139

Silence expresses the wonder of spiritualization. It is a force, a constitutive and ontological principle distinct from but associated with other forces such as spirit and word, in the constitution of the human world. It is this kind of silence, the unexpressed communication, that finds unique expression among the Igbo.

The Igbo are very effervescent, vivacious and gregarious, very ebullient, extroverted and loquacious, especially in their greetings and day-to-day interactions (Mbabuike, 1991). They interact openly even with complete strangers. Greeting is very boisterous and generously exchanged at all times and places. No matter how many times one passes by another at any given time, it is expected that greetings be exchanged. Refusal to exchange greetings indicates a strained relationship.

Normally, it is the younger person who first extends greetings to the older. In a situation where the younger person fails to initiate greeting, the older would sarcastically greet the younger. Then he would ask questions like, *bia nwam, i budi nwa onye?* (Come here, my child, who is your father? or who are your parents?). He would take the complaint to the child's parents. Of course, the child receives serious reprimand.

In Houston, when they gather for the festivals, just like in their ancestral land, they unleash such unrestricted exuberance, exchanging loud and extravagant greetings. Discussions are loud and long. They cheer, applaud, scream, clap, and jump.

When they dance, they exhibit such energy-filled stamina, such kinetic flair, stomping and stamping, spinning and swirling, rocking and pivoting with agility, strength, and elasticity. They maintain their footwork with such percussive animism, causing their rattles to shake and agitate in ecstatic frenzy. Their exuberance and effervescence are even manifested in the rustling of their costumes, the dangling of their pendants, necklaces, and earrings, the chiming and clanking of the wristlets and anklets as they walk.

They also use many loud-sounding, head-pounding, ear-piercing instruments---the horns that pierce through the tight, silent air; the drums that beat and beat and beat, raising music to fever pitch; the bells that ring again and again and again to a sonorous tintinnabulation, signaling the arrival of the visitors from the land of the dead. Above this background of exuberance hovers a mysterious thick, dark cloud of silence that descends at intervals, like a heavy thunderstorm, and floods their world.

This silence manifests during rituals, when the physical world must give way for the advent of the Superhuman. At such times, the entire place is filled with silence, conjuring images that are complex, yet vivid and capable of catapulting one into a world where silent voices whisper peace, assurance, life, health and prosperity. At funerals, such silence becomes the eloquence of the unspoken.

When the Igbo visit a bereaved family, all that noise disappears. Nobody says anything to anybody. The visitors, with hands across their chests, on their heads or behind their backs, simply walk straight to the bereaved family, stand there for a while (maybe until their presence is recognized), and then, as quietly as they came in, they take their seats among other mourners (Mbabuike, 1991).

After staying for as long as they wish to stay, they walk quietly back to the bereaved, repeat the process of silent sympathy, concern and show of presence and, as silently as they had come in, they take their leave. "Thus speech, the characterizing signature of humanity, has been superseded by silence to communicate unspoken experience beyond the limitation of human consciousness, such as fear, longing, and death" (Kane, 1984, p. 12).

Davidson (1971) records such mysterious image of silence on the death of a great wrestler in another African community:

> ...*Grief sweeps the community. Thousands of tribesmen pour into the village to pay their last respects.... While mourners file past the athlete, his fellow wrestlers intone a prayer.... Outside the hut, dancers move in stunned silence (p. 75).*

This type of silence is such that evokes the image of the posture of one who listens attentively to the messages of a higher order. It is such that evokes an image of dark forces that allow the will no recourse and induces a strong mystic and linguistic isolation. It is the state in which the spirit suppresses all verbal expression and becomes a fertile ground for the advent of the superhuman, the state of melancholy, of ominous splendor and of breathless, empty stillness. It dwells in quiet wisdom. It is stillness eloquent of something. It is a new life on a superhuman plane, which lies beyond the realm of language.

Dauenheuer (1980) speaks of such life. He describes it as a life where silent images whisper profound secrets, the secrets of humanity's innermost being. It is the ascending ladder, which connects the material world with the spiritual, giving the soul the inevitable extension and transcendence, and carrying it to the realm of pure light. George Steiner describes it as a realm of ever-deepening taciturnity (Ryan, 1988).

It is this silence that permeates the total being of the Igbo artist as he creates his art, keeping him in communion with the ancestors---the eloquent silence of awe, the unspeakable silence of ritual, the ominous silence of darkness. Umezinwa (1980) notes how Chinua Achebe allows his readers the privilege of seeing an Igbo carver, Edogo, at work in *Arrow of God*:

> *Hidden in the spirit house, Edogo made conscious efforts at finishing the carving of a mask for a new ancestral spirit. "Now and again, he heard the voices of people passing through the market place from one village of Umuaro to another." After a while, his conscious efforts left him. "But when his carving finally got hold of him, he heard no more voices" (p. 20).*

It is the same silence that permeates the children's world as they are engaged in creative activity, putting them in constant communion with the unknown voices of the cosmos, the spirits that wield the brushes, the pencils, the pastels, and the pens with the Creator's precision. It is the same silence, the original stillness that permeated the universe in the beginning, during creation.

Such silences transform everyday objects into mute symbols in an attempt to get at the occult voices of heaven. Alastair (1978) describes it as that which opens the empty crepuscular space of one's own familiar interior.

Achebe (1958) illustrates this silence in an Igbo folk tale about Mother Kite and the duck in another novel, *Things Fall Apart* when Mother Kite sent her daughter to bring food. The first food she brought was a duckling. For the fact that the mother of the duckling did not say a word, Mother Kite asked her daughter to return the duckling to her mother because "there is something ominous behind the silence" (p. 130).

Soon, Daughter Kite brought another food. This time, it was a chick.

When Mother Kite asked her daughter what the mother of the chick said, she replied, "It cried and raved and cursed me."

"Then we can eat the chick," said her mother. "There is nothing to fear from someone who shouts" (p. 130).

Silence thus has a potential power of expressiveness, which manages highly charged situations and relationships. It is an eloquence of the inarticulate. In his 1899 Manifesto, Symons vividly states this immense ritualistic attribute of silence. He describes silence as an endeavor to revolt against exteriority, against rhetoric, against materialistic tradition, an endeavor to disengage the ultimate essence, the soul, of whatever exists (Kane, 1984).

Thus, when the Igbo artist secludes himself in the forest in readiness for his job, he feels emotionally content in the twilight state between total awareness and total oblivion, a state of silent listening in which he feels closest to the secrets of the invisible realm, feeling the silent presence of Mother Nature. It is a situation so captivating, so intimate, so consummating, so profound, so personal.

Goldwater (1979) describes such a situation as a condition through which the artist could ignore the material and thus be able to penetrate the spiritual and

143

communicate with the unknown voices of heaven, the occult voices of the spirits, which can only be heard in silence. It is the type of silence that creates space within which the gods may work.

Hence, the Igbo artist isolates himself in order to capture that uninterrupted moment, shutting out appearances in order to concentrate upon essence; to recreate an inward experience that cannot be achieved by discursive thought. Such moment is the type that Gauguin depicted in his painting, "Christ in Gethsemane" 1889. Here, he uses isolation to achieve the silence utilized in capturing the inner experience of Christ.

Christ's withdrawal to isolation was in quest for silence, which would create the desired mood needed to delve into the spiritual realm in order to be in communion with God. It was a withdrawal in search for solitude, a solitude, which cultivates silence, the silence geared toward spiritual satisfaction, the spirit, which can only be overheard in silence.

It is only in absolute silence that spiritual voices become clear, and it is this silent clarity, attentive to those forces hidden beneath the surface of the common-place, that Christ Himself sought. It is this same silence that Gauguin depicts. It is the same that the Igbo artist seeks.

Auchard (1986) describes such communion as a mutual attentiveness which is most often evoked as a resonance of Nature in man and man in Nature --- Nature which communes with the inner man, the heart, the soul, the feelings, those faculties whose functioning beyond speech constitute a higher eloquence.

This powerful silence, this dumb silence of apathy, this sober silence of solemnity, transcends cultural and even religious boundaries. Christian and non-Christian orders, regardless of the conception of highest authority, are replete with silence in an attempt to capture a high spiritual elevation. Even God's appearances to His prophets in the Bible are in still, small voices --- in the wilderness with John the Baptist, in the brook with Elijah, in the burning bushes with Moses, in Gethsemane with Jesus, and with others in lonely places, on mountain tops.

The still, small voice whispers silence, the silence of inner religious experience, the experience of the little boy Samuel, the experiences of Abraham, Isaac and Jacob, the experiences of Joseph and Moses, the experiences of Elijah and Elisha, the experience of Jesus Himself in the Garden. It was the same experience that Gauguin depicts in "Christ in Gethsemane" 1889. Tannen and Saville-Troike (1985) declare that such situations presented through silence are the most efficacious of human experiences.

In Igbo, when masquerades perform, they exhibit some kinetic energy. No matter how old the performer is, he acquires, almost immediately, youthful exuberance with much added agility and elasticity. He finds comfort in the "fluidity of silence which allows him journey to the depths of the psyche, to exteriorize, dramatize and emphasize what the symbolists call 'Letat d'ame' " (Kane, 1984, p.14) (the state of the soul). It is this same temptation and authority of silence as a means of expressing the unspoken and the unspeakable that the Igbo evoke in funerals.

Silence involves the struggle between the body and the imagination. It is a combination of images, which are plural, complex, and ambiguous. It is that which leads from the visible to the invisible, and from the invisible to the illusion of appearances as perceived by man.

In his "Vision After the Sermon", Gauguin uses this theme of silence to successfully manipulate and control a somewhat bizarre situation. The subjects in this painting are in a meditative mood. Gauguin positioned them in such a way that the viewer is kept out of the picture, to avoid interruption or disruption of that spiritual experience, the experience that is possible only in silence. Their eyes and mouths are closed; their palms are put together in meditative quiescence. The entire scene breathes silence, the prelude to holiness, the embodiment of the totality of spiritual communion.

Silence creates images that call to mind the Christmas carol, "Silent Night." Here, two forces are put together to create an amazingly wonder-filled moment. It was night; therefore impenetrably dark. It was silent; therefore, unspeakably quiet. It was a silent night; therefore a Holy night. All was calm. The birds were not singing; the insects were not creaking. The world was quiet, asleep. It was during this night, this silent night that God Himself came down and became human.

Darkness therefore becomes a prelude to silence and silence a prelude to divine holiness, a bridge between two worlds --- the world of the supernatural and the world of humanity. But for the Igbo, darkness breeds silent terror

Types of Silence

Silence is so inseparably woven into the fabric of Igbo culture that it is difficult to speak of the Igbo without silent images. Achebe used silent images many times, more than fifty times, in *Things Fall Apart* such that the story would not have been complete without them. The novel speaks of "the deathly silence," "the complete silence," "the intense and vibrant silence," "the speechless silence," "the perfect silence," "the silence of anticipation," "the pulsating silence of tirelessness." It conjures the images of "the silent walk to the shrine," "the throbbing silence of the Evil Forest," "the descending silence that swallows the noise," and on and on and on.

These types of silences, said Kane (1984) "'illustrate by their unspoken response to speech that experiences exist for which we lack words" (p 15). Silence, therefore, plays a vital role in Igbo art and culture, and to understand the art of the Igbo, one must understand its silence.

It is expedient to point out at this juncture that Igbo sculptures, like other African sculptures, with all their power and authority take the posture of restfulness, standing or sitting in repose. This is so because, as Schmalenbach

(1988) observes, "their activity is of another order than that of the human body" (p.18).

This is also true of Igbo mask. Its power is within, and it exercises it in silence --- the muzzled silence of impasse, the silence more eloquent than any known word, the silence more powerful than any force known to human. This silence is often reflected in the closed eyes of the carved masks, which suggests some internality, spirituality and serenity. Sometimes the eyes of the masks are pierced to reflect or express some inner agitation, some intrinsic unrest. The images which silence creates could appear odd, curious, and strange, articulating the unspeakable.

Igbo artists, therefore, cultivate silence to evoke the image of God, the God who dwells alone, silently, above the world, to express a wonder of spiritualization; of pure movement, pure coming to expression, thus serving the innate divinely ordained necessity-- the necessity to interact with the spirit, the spirit which is God. It is this kind of silence, the unexpressed communication, the unspeakable mystery of the divine that could be found among the Igbo of West Africa and their art.

CHAPTER 11

Theater and the Art of the Igbo

One of the original concepts of Igbo theater is to re-emphasize and re-establish the beliefs of the people. Like the indigenous African theater, it serves a purpose within communities and cultures that is much greater than simply that of entertainment or diversion (Banham and Wake, 1976). It is ritualistic and religious, a means of communication. During one of the festivals observed, the Chief Ritualist stood to speak.

He spoke in the native dialect. He cleared his throat as if to call the people's attention to him:

Ndi eze, Kelenu!	The chiefs, I greet you
Ndi ozo, Kelenu!	Titled men, I greet you
Umu Igbo, Kwenu!	The Igbo, I salute you
Ihe anyi biara ime bu omenala.	We are here to perform our custom
Onye o bula gee nti nke oma	Listen very attentively
Ka m kpokuo ndi ichie____	I'll call on the ancestors____
Ndi Ichie	Our Ancestors
Ndi nnanna anyi ha	Our forefathers
Ala Igbo	The land of the Igbo
Ala America	The land of America
Ndewonu!	I salute you
Ebe anyi siri bia di anya	Our home is far away
Kama, Chi anyi na-edu anyi.	But, our God is our guide
O biara nga onye abiagbula ya	Let the visitor not bring death to host
Ya lawa, nkpunkpu apula ya	And when he leaves, do so in peace
Egbe bere; Ugo bere	Let the Kite perch; let the Egret perch also.

149

For the Igbo, the ancestors are the source of strength and power. They call on them first before doing anything else. Their life will not be complete without them. Igbo ancestors are a part of a continuum of existence which *Ala* (Mother Earth) also forms a part. For the Igbo, life force and existence force form a continuum between life and death---a circle of existence.

As stated earlier, the ancestors are the intercessors. They are a part of the spiritual governance that takes care of the people and of things. They are to the Igbo what the Patron Saints are to the Christians. At this point, the Chief Ritualist was attempting to re-establish and re-emphasize their belief, to communicate with the ancestors, and to do so requires that they give their undivided attention.

His silence seemed to convey a serene sense of spiritual transcendence. He looked blankly at the crowd---looking at them, but seeing something else. His posture evoked the image of one who listens attentively to the messages of a higher order. It was the type of silence, which transforms everyday objects into mute symbols in an attempt to get at the occult voices of heaven. It was the type that opens up the empty twilight zone of one's own familiar interior.

He recognized the land that they are presently on (the land of America), signifying that *Ala* (Mother Earth) is the same all over the world. It is the awareness that their ancestors are attached to Mother Earth; hence wherever land is, the ancestors are there also.

So when he poured the drink on the American soil, he was certain that the ancestors would receive it because, as the Igbo say, a message sent through the smoke will definitely reach the sky. This drama was an attempt to tap the vital energy that controls life, an attempt to make the invisible visible and the intangible tangible.

In Amadi's (1973) play, *Isiburu*, the actors perform such rituals to solicit the guidance and protection of the gods of the land. In Igbo culture, the gods are served first before anyone else. Such ritual is performed at different occasions and places, most of the time in the shrines of the gods, which house their carved images. Such rituals are also performed in monologue.

The audience's participation during the monologue is minimal, but its silence is evocative of something spiritual...a concentration upon the unseen and the unheard which suggests a mysterious reality beyond appearance. "This ritual theater", Soyinka (1976) notes, "viewed from the spatial perspective, aims to reflect through physical and symbolic means the archetypal struggle of the mortal being against exterior forces" (p. 43).

Igbo theater, as will be used in this study, does not fit the Western definition of theater in its actual sense. It will be pointless to conceive of it as drama in a Shakespearean sense. For the purpose of this study, Igbo theater will be viewed from the perspective of African traditional festival---a ritual drama which Ogunba (1978) says "brings to life all the ancestors, the gods and all the heavenly crew in their various forms to jubilate with man for the completion of another cycle of events, to help him purify his environment and remind him of his duties....

It is this peculiar chain of communications, this complex earth-heaven dynamic relationship that traditional African drama is about" (p. 9). It must first be made crystal clear that "African traditional festivals are not an orgy of merriment or a string of weird, primitive sacrifices and dances as most writers foreign to African culture portray them to be" (Ogunba, 1974, p. 4).

Even most educated Africans who have lost contact with their roots, who have sold their birthrights for a bowl of porridge, who are confused and trapped in a tug-of-war of different cultures, are most guilty of this misconception. They are like the little bird, "*nza*", in Achebe's (1959) *Things Fall Apart*, who forgot himself after a heavy meal and challenged his *chi* (personal god) or the hunter's dog that suddenly goes mad and turns on his master.

One thing is certain, however; although those alienated Africans are educated, they are uninitiated. Since these "little birds" and, to quote Graham-White (1974) directly, "members of an alien people, have not been initiated into the cult or society to which the performance or mask belongs, its religious significance may well be deliberately withheld from them", therefore, to them, "the ritual, the mask, the masquerade, or the dance loses the sacred power it derived from its religious associations" (p. 20). That is the difference, and it is a significant difference.

African festival is a ritual dramatic performance. It is, as Ogunba (1974) states, "an integral, dynamic part of the culture of an un-alienated African, an occasion to which he responds spontaneously" (p. 4). It was to such an occasion that an initiated African artist in the United States, very far away from home, responded:

>It's Halloween again, and it's that time of the year when spirits, malevolent and benevolent, demand attention. I'm beginning to feel my head swell, gradually, like a solitary walker in the darkness, on a narrow, winding forest path.
>
>I'm beginning to feel my stomach turn over, slowly, gradually, like a porpoise in deep water. I'm beginning to sense the presence of the spirits even here and now, millions of miles away from home.
>
>I can hear them whisper in my ears. In the distance, I can hear the flutes sing, the ogene sound, and the drums beat, rising and falling in an awe-inspiring crescendo, serenading the living and the dead.
>I feel the power!
>I feel it now!
>Wow!
>Wield those drumsticks!
>Beat that drum!
>Beat it!
>Beat it hard!
>I hear you!
>I understand!
>My mouth foams!
>I leave my homework undone!
>I leave my food untasted!
>Ekpe!
>Mboko!
>Ezumezu!
>Ofo!
>Forgive me folks. Some of you may not understand. A few of you may. This is not "trick or treat." It's do or die. It's for real. Children don't run around with baskets of candies. They are

*indoors somewhere, peeping through any available hole to catch a
glimpse of the men.*
*The women and the uninitiated men hide behind closed
doors, wondering and wishing. The initiated own the ground now,
and they parade it with pride and dignity, singing and dancing and
waiting for the masquerade to appear from the land of the spirit.*

Masquerading is a very important aspect of this ritual drama. It
coordinates all the art forms of the community, including costumes, masking,
drumming, chanting, and dancing, and, as Ogunba (1974) notes, "and when one
watches a traditional African festival, one is immediately struck by the fact that
one has been exposed to a dramatic experience" (p. 9).

It is from this perspective of ritual dramatic performance that the Igbo
theater will be viewed. This whole concept of ritual drama---a physical and
metaphysical representation of religion---includes any spirit-filled performance
involving an audience and fits quite well with Kirby's (1974) definition of African
theater---the representation of another being or character by a performer for an
audience. It will be pertinent to point out at the outset that the initial perspective
assumed by this study does not suggest that Igbo drama operates only on this
level.

For the Igbo, theater is a ritual, a collective, religious phenomenon,
capable of awakening in the recess of the spirit the things, which the whole
community cares about. It is, as in their art, spirit-regarding. In support of this
concept, Ogunba (1978) writes:

> *The whole performance appears geared toward
> transcending humanity or the natural order; that is, to create
> larger than life-size characters who put on other-worldly
> appearances, speak the strange language of spirits, stride between
> heaven and earth or between the abode of water spirits and land
> with ease, and at the end of it all, dance through to possession;
> that is, to a standard acceptable to the supernatural patrons (p.
> 12).*

153

This ritual, this religious phenomenon, this silent communication with the cosmos, is the root of Igbo drama and performance. Such dramatic performances will be categorized as ritual, spirit-cult and masquerades, involving different and diverse theatrical elements such as masks and costumes, movement and dance, music and song, mime and character.

Ritual and Spirit-Cult Performance

Rituals form the warp on which the tapestry of culture is woven (Mclaren, 1986). Kirby (1974) describes ritual as "a series of actions designed to achieve a magical effect" (p. 24). Among the Igbo, ritual is an attempt to tap the vital energy that controls life, an attempt to make the invisible visible, and the intangible tangible.

Rituals are performed during different occasions and for diverse purposes. Graham-White (1974) notes that some rituals are non-dramatic while some employ some elements of drama, which includes impersonation, dialogue, conflict, and plot.

Among the Igbo, ritual performances are complex, consisting of highly emotionally charged, spirit-filled performances that require systematic staging, and involve the offering of sacrifices to gods and ancestors. Such rituals contain a variety of acts equivalent to drama and are performed during New Yam festivals, harvests, before planting season, and before and after hunting expeditions.

Yam: The King of Crops

Yam in Igboland is the king of crops. It is a sacred symbol around which centers much of Igbo religious life. The sanctity of yam is manifested in the Igbo belief that yam cannot be stolen either from the farm or from the barn. Such an offense is punishable by death. *Ala* (Mother Earth) nurtures the yam planted on the land while *Igwe* (the sky god) waters it.

The feast of the new yam is a time when the Igbo give thanks to Ala, the earth goddess, who is believed to be the source of all fertility and the ultimate

154

judge of morality and conduct (Achebe, 1959). At harvest time, for example, the oldest member of the family or a priest performs the ritual. The procedure varies according to the extent of sacrifice and solicitation.

After preparing the new yams for dinner, before anybody could taste them, the entire family or village gather around the shrine of an ancestor or *Ifejioku*, the god of yams. The priest stands before the shrine and delivers a monologue in form of incantations. He offers kolanut, fresh palm-wine, blood of a slaughtered rooster, pieces of the new yam and cooked chicken while the audience watches with heightened belief and anticipation that all is or will be well:

Chukwu Abiama	God Almighty
Abassi di n'elu	God in Heaven
Nke a bu ji, rie	This is yam, eat
Nke a bu anu, taa	This is meat, eat
Nke a bu mmanya,	This is wine
Ndu ogologo	Long life
Ahu ike	Good health
Nke a bu ekpere anyi	This is our prayer
Nna anyi ha	Our fathers
Ndi ichie	The ancestors
Werenu nke a	Take this

Then he takes another piece of yam, waves it on each person's head two times and gives that piece to *Ala*, the queen of the underworld who is in close communion with the departed fathers of the clan whose bodies had been committed to earth (Achebe, 1959).

When the Igbo in Houston observed the festival of the New Yam, the Chief Ritualist performed the rituals:

This is the most important aspect of our being, and, of course, the most important aspect of this occasion. We are about to go to the spirit-house. We ask that our visitors who may not be able to understand to please bear with us. I will go back to the native tongue, because the ritual that I am about to perform cannot be done in a foreign language.

Igbo, Kwenu!
Igbo, Kwenu!
Bende, Kwenu!
Kwezuenu!

After each greeting the crowd responded with a resounding, *Yaah!* He held
up a plate full of kolanut.

Oji Igbo anaghi aga njem.
(Kolanut in Igboland doesn't travel.)

Ewerela m oji a zi nde Umuahia
(I've shown the kolanut to Umuahia)

Ewerela m oji a zi nde Ikwuano
(I've shown the kolanut to Ikwuano)

Nde Nkpa, Nkporo, Abiriba,
(To Nkpa, Nkporo, Abiriba)

Abam, Umuhu, Ututu, Arochukwu, Abam, Umuhu, Ututu,
Arochukwu, *Ihechiowa, Umunnato, Alayi, Item*, Umunnato, Alayi,
Item, *Ozuitem na Igbere.*

He walked to the center of the hall, held up one of the kolanuts. *(Silence).*

Ndi ichie Bende, unu were oji
(Ancestors of Bende, here's kolanut).

Ndi ichie Igbo, Unu were oji
(Ancestors of Igbo, here's kolanut).

Ndi ichie Nigeria, unu were oji
(Ancestors of Nigeria, here's kolanut.)

Ndi ichie Africa, unu were oji
(Ancestor of Africa, here's kolanut)
Onye choro ihe oma, ihe oma biara ya.
(Grant peace to the peacemaker)

Ndu ogolologo
(Long life)

156

Omumu
(Offsprings)

Aku na uba
(Prosperity)

Udo na onu
(Peace and joy)

He broke the kolanut, tossed the pieces on the floor and walked back to his seat. The crowd was dead silent. He picked up a bottle of wine or some type of drink in a bottle:

> Our ancestors cannot take half measures. We have given them kolanut. We must also give them drink. I must complete this ceremony so that when I go home tonight, I can sleep well in my bed.

He walked to the center of the hall again.

> *Ndi ichie Bende*
> (The ancestors of Bende)
> *Ndi ichie Igbo*
> (The ancestors of Igbo)
> *Ndi ichie Nigeria*
> (The ancestors of Nigeria)
> *Ndi ichie Africa*
> (The ancestors of Africa)
> *Unu lee mmanya*
> (This wine is for you)

He poured some of the contents of the bottle on the floor three times and walked back to his seat. Then he said:

> Now, everyone can eat the kolanut and drink. We have pleased our ancestors, and we know that they will in turn please us. This time, we are going to experience the best. We are waiting for the arrival of our ancestors from the spirit world. Please, mothers, hold your children. *Okonko* is coming!

The Chief Ritualist expressed that the ritual he was about to perform could not be done in a foreign language. This is not because the ancestors do not understand a foreign language. They are spirits, and they can understand any language. However, in order to attain proximity and claim relationship beyond distance, that language which the living shared with the dead must be used.

Perhaps this explains why some of the worship rituals in Catholic churches are done in Latin---a language readily understood by the living and the departed saints. The fact of the matter is that the Igbo have established a communication pattern with their ancestors over the years, which makes it possible for the information to flow easily. Also, there are some elements of the language that are not always easily translatable into a foreign language.

In Igbo, as in every other African culture, ritual and spirit-cult performances take different forms. During such performances, persons are possessed by spirits, and during the time of possession, they are no longer themselves. The spirit takes complete control, and they begin to speak in esoteric voices and act the part of the spirit. When the spirits appear, they bring with them a range of feelings, from moments of psychic shock, of terror, of mortal danger, to moments of fascination, of inspiration, of admiration.

The degree of possession is so great that the individual is transformed, and he finds himself in a pathological state of trance. As soon as the spirit takes control, new energy comes into the person-spirit such that even an old person who ordinarily wobbles now begins to stamp, stomp, tumble, swirl, roll and jump, exhibiting such intensive kinetic flair, such speed, such agility, such elasticity with such vital rhythmic impulse. He maintains his footwork with consummate vitality, and his body with percussive strength. His appearance changes

During *okonko* or *ekpe* or *mboko* (spirit-cult ritual performances), the initiated parade the ground. They are in charge. The uninitiated and the women sit in designated areas in the *ama* (the village playground), and watch from a distance bared with *omu* (tender palm fronds). When the *okonko* or *ekpo* masquerade appears, a resounding roar echoes through the air.

Gunshots herald the appearance of the spirit from the land of the ancestors. The drums beat, the flutes sing, and the spectators watch in transfixed mixture of awe and admiration. Such appearances, Thompson (1974) notes, "bring pleasure precisely because many people see the founders of the nation or lineage returning in these styles" (p. 44). As Graham-White (1974) also adds, "they transport the participants into a world in which actions escape from the logic of everyday experience, actions whose rules the participants must accept in advance" (p.16).

Igbo Art in Motion

The appearance of the spirit is a spectacular sight. The colorful, rustling costumes, the awe-inspiring mask, the dangling bells and rattles, and all that chime, ring, and clank, accentuate the gestures of his movement and add to the head-swelling, heart-pounding and breathtaking sensations experienced by the audience.

Suspension of disbelief does not apply. To everybody involved, what is happening is real. They are beholding the ancient elders being reunited again in the bodies of the dancers and the masks (Thompson 1974).

During one of their appearances observed here in Houston, the masquerades brought with them the same pleasure, the same joy, and the same excitement. The total feeling was nothing short of nostalgia. One could sense the heightened anticipation in the eyes of the people. They anticipated the appearance of the *okonko*, but the nature of its appearance remained hidden from them until the actual manifestation.

Even the elders seemed anxious. Those who were sitting behind taller people stood up, peering toward the anticipated direction from which the *okonko* would emerge. A bell rang from a distance, then closer, closer, and closer, then it

159

became sonorous. All was silent. In the midst of this large crowd, one could hear a pin drop.

A man dressed in short, red, green and white striped skirt walked in, holding a bell in one hand and a rattle metal in the other. A line of white chalk ran across his eyes. His chest, arms, legs were all painted with white chalk. The rattles in his ankles shook to his solid, steady steps. He walked straight to the table where the elders and the Ritual lord were sitting, stopped, struck his metal rattle once on the floor, rang the bell one more time, adjusted the yellow ostrich feather on his red cap, turned around, shook his bare chest and walked his way back to where he had come from.

Moments later, the drums began to beat; first it was distant, then close, then closer. Six drummers came in, already perspiring. It seemed like they had been playing for hours in the sun. They were all dressed like the herald. They walked to a corner of the open space, sat down on the chairs provided for them and continued. People cheered, but their eyes were still gazing at the entrance.

A horn sounded, piercing through the music. Two young children came in, dancing to the beat of the intricate rhythm of the drums. The lead drummer's hands began to move rapidly, raising the music to fever pitch. Soon shouts emanated within the dressing room. The bell rang, again and again. The Okonko appeared, jumping and stomping with the agility of a leopard, the strength of a tiger, the majesty of a lion and the elasticity of a cat. The silence of anticipation gave way to the exuberance of reunion and certainty.

Seconds later, another Okonko followed, then another and another. The hall broke apart. People cheered and screamed. The Okonko swirled and stamped. The rattles and bells on their waists shook in ecstatic frenzy. People surged forward as if to behold the dancing visitors from the underworld. The elders stood up and joined them.

The Ritual lord waved his staff in the air in jubilation. He danced to the drummers, threw money on them, danced to the Okonko and threw money on

160

them one by one. The elders followed. Others in the crowd who wished to throw money came out, dancing and spraying money. It was a total celebration.

Masquerading

The essence of this study lies in the ineluctable fact that masquerade epitomizes the art of the Igbo. It is, as Kirby (1974) notes, the representative form of African indigenous theater. It is the nerve center of Igbo culture. Achebe (1984) expresses this view very well:

> *Of all the art forms the dance and the masquerade would*
> *appear to have satisfied the Igbo artistic appetite most completely.*
> *They subsume all forms of the arts --- sculpture, music, painting,*
> *drama, costume and even*
> *architecture* (p. ix).

They are the source of communication with the ancestors and the gods of the land. They originate from ritual and performances of the secret society.

The secret society acts as the executive agent while the masquerade is the judiciary. Schmalenback (1988) notes that masqueraders do not pretend to represent other beings; they are such beings. They are not human beings hiding behind a mask to disguise themselves for trick or treat.

Masquerading involves strenuous, physical activity: jumping, stomping, dancing, whirling, and all. In fact, it is the movement, the dance, and, of course, the costumes that give life to the mask. As Achebe (1984) adds, it is this artistic deployment of motion, agility and elasticity that informs the Igbo concept of existence.

Schmalenbach (1988) observes that "even the masks, for all their greater vitality and fantasy, are essentially static; indeed, they appear all the more rigid in the midst of the violent movements of the dance" (p.18). "It is the dance," says Laude (1978) "that sets off the process of elucidating, perpetuating, and transferring knowledge...a knowledge of cosmic order" (p. 18).

161

Although masquerades vary from one village community to the other, the underlying principles are the same. They embody the reincarnated spirits of the ancestors and represent a range of human experience. Achebe (1984) recalls seeing different types of masquerades as a boy growing up in Ogidi, an Igbo village. He speaks of masquerades that range from youth to old age and from playfulness to terror. He speaks of the *Agbogho mmuo* (the maiden spirit) mask with its delicate beauty and the *Njo ka Oya* with its disease-like ugliness.

Aniakor and Cole (1984) also note a different range of masquerades. They speak of masquerades with powerful authorities and sanctions to judge or even kill. They speak about masquerades that stomp and float, and masquerades that swirl and stamp.

There are a host of others that are worth mentioning, some of which have made appearances in the United States. These include the *Okiti* of Ozubulu whose gigantic gaping teeth and fierce physical features convulse the onlooker and the *Okwoli* of Oko whose esoteric voice beckons on the living and the dead.

Other masquerades include the *Nwanyiotulaukwu* of Otampa that incarnate every other year to reassure the community of its well-being and unity, the *Ajonkwu* of Ovim that sizzles with agility and elasticity, tumbling, jumping and cutting down palm-fronds and heads of goats in one quick slice, the sensational *Ebi* of Umuobiala that rattle and chime and jingle, the *Ukwom* of Amaibo, the *Okperegede* of Izzi and Ikwo, the *Ijele* of Achalla and Aguleri, the *Ikperikpeogu* of Bende, the *Ojionu* masquerade of Ndizuogu. The list could go on and on and on.

Just as Achebe (1984) was quick to point out, none of these masquerades mentioned here could do justice to a host of others not mentioned. It might be of interest to point out that the few mentioned immediately above are from the researchers own community, some of which he has had the unique and exceptional privilege of experiencing as an initiated Igbo.

The intensive and vigorous theatrical performances of these spirits of the ancestors are caught and expressed in the magical formulas of art, in mask

162

carving, which, d'Azevedo (1973) admits, comprises an intricate set of man's activities, touching upon many sides of man. He describes it as a set of overlapping circles with several centers.

The Igbo mask performs the function of liberating the actor into the character. It eliminates the individuality and replaces it with a stimulation of action. It deals with the relation of man to those supernatural, divine powers which are sometimes felt to be irrational, sometimes cruel, and sometimes just, and reveals, in one way or another, man's belief in his nature and destiny and the nature of the world he inhabits (the seen and the unseen), rather than just an entertainment forum.

The "actor", the masquerader, must submit himself totally to the charge of the spirit he is evoking. He must let go his ego so that the god may appear. He frees himself from the known outer forms of daily life and taps into a deeper lying stream of energy, of vitality, of elasticity, of agility.

Once the soul of the ancestor possesses the soul of the wearer, the latter is no longer himself. He begins to speak in an unintelligible jargon (Messenger, 1973) and explodes with a rapture of energy and undiminished stamina, transcending the pathos of mortality. He closes his eyes, bulges them enormously, or rolls the pupils to an uncanny glitter. He freezes his face or expands his cheek with balloon-like elasticity.

Sometimes he gapes his teeth or thrusts out his tongue, depending on the deity in control. It is the same ecstatic dispositions that the artist tries to depict in the masks portraying these deities.

The transformation begins, like mysteries, in silence, the somber silence that agitates the soul; the deepening taciturnity that holds the audience in the suspense of the possible and sweeps its feet in rapture. Whereas the Igbo artist (the mask carver) strives to create an abode for a spirit, the actor (the mask dancer) strives to exorcise the spirit through his actions, his movement, and his gestures (Thompson, 1974).

163

The artist (the mask carver) breathes silent heat and energy into the mask. It is this silent heat, this silent energy, this silent roar, this silent pulse that ruptures into a percussive vitality during performance. This is the reason the carver is not completely satisfied with a mask until he sees it in motion, in action, in performance, and costume plays a vital role in this ensemble.

Masks form a part of the costumes, and they cannot be fully understood and appreciated when isolated from the costumes. As Laude (1978) states, they need to be considered in the context of the whole complex and spectacular ensemble for which they were made.

Ritual, even more than in social or secular occasions, demonstrates the importance of costume in Igbo culture. Through elaboration and specialization, attire defines specific roles within cult groups. In masquerade, as well as in ritual context, appropriate costume is extremely important.

Picton and Mack (1979) observe that African ritual costumes are used "for the manifestations of the world of the dead, or some other mode of existence in masquerade form" (p. 10). One of the functions of the mask is to stabilize and absorb the energy released during sacrifices, and costumes and dance form an integral part of this activity (Laude, 1978).

The masked dancers wear long costumes that cover their entire body. This is intended to protect them from the dangerous spell of the wandering spirits.

Masquerades that perform to commemorate a deceased elder wear costumes designed to incorporate relics of the deceased man it commemorates. When a person dies, certain energy is released. If left unchecked, this could cause disaster to the community, thus, it must be trapped and controlled.

Cole and Aniakor (1984) also point out that many prestigious and powerful masked spirits may not dance without ritual preparations of masks, costumes, wearer, and environment in order to insure the success of their outing. Every mask has a specific rhythm (Video tape). If a dancer cannot perform the steps, it is assumed that the spirit is not in control.

A good example is the *Nwanyiotulaukwu* (the woman with big buttocks) masquerade of Otampa. This masquerade has to dance to the steps assigned to the particular spirit or the dancer will be led to the spirit house and unmasked. Thompson (1974) notes that even "the player on the *ekwe* (wooden gong) orchestrates the quick stops and thrusting pulsations, shaping the asymmetrical, explosive gestures of the mask" (p. 164).

Most personal adornment in ritual context focuses on the head. This is because the head is believed to be the seat of man's life. It is also an object of cult. As Cordwell and Schwarz (1979) note, "it is the place where the spirit of a god enters or mounts the devotee during rites of possession" (p. 192). In most instances, the head is covered and extended by means of headdresses.

The covering of the head and eyes finds its richest expression in masquerades directed toward powerful spiritual entities, the gods and ancestors which the Igbo proudly refer to as *Chi nnanna anyi ha* (the gods of our forefathers). These gods are believed to be responsible for the existence of the universe. It is this belief in mystical powers that has influenced the totality of their art and way of life.

Summary

The music and dances of the Igbo are much more than theatrical entertainment; they have a religious content, and are an expression of the very essence of African life. They embody the totality of the fabric of the people's culture. Music and dance are always present in the ritual ceremonies of the Igbo as a very distinctive feature of their culture.

Music and dance come to play during harvests, initiations and marriage ceremonies. They are accompanied by masks and are carried out to the rhythm of the drum, the blowing of the horn, and the tinkling of iron bells. "Together, the sculpture, the dances, the drum music and the songs," said Davidson (1971), "reinforce the workings of the force within nature that animates all life...the creative energy from which all blessings flow" (p.145).

CHAPTER 12

The Search for Meaning

The Igbo gather almost every weekend to celebrate their culture and embark on projects to help their families in their homeland. These gatherings are not only colorful and spectacular, but they also inform and educate.

The Gathering

The cultural gathering was scheduled to begin by 8:00 p.m. At about 8:30 p.m., people started coming in. The very first spectacular sight was their costumes. It took no effort to sense in the wearers the glow of secure self-esteem. Although the elements of the costumes varied from person to person, the overall impression was one of beauty and grandeur, one of richness of culture, a positive sense of identity and pride.

The Costumes

The men's costumes varied considerably from the women's. The men adorned themselves in a complicated assemblage of garments. They appeared to exhibit a serene sense of self-assurance, which seemed to result from knowledge of their status as men combined with an awareness of occasion. Most of the men wore caps on their heads which appeared to be made of leopard skin, some of brocade - green, red, white, blue and a combination of other colors.

There were others who wore hats, which appeared to be concocted of a variety of materials, ranging from leather to the most expensive of materials decorated with cowry shells, beads, and feathers. Some of the hats were sewn,

167

stitched, plaited; others were woven, crocheted and appliquéd and elaborately embroidered.

Most of the men came with carved wooden staffs. Some of the staffs (or working sticks) had elephant heads carved on them; some had lion heads, while some were simply plain. Almost all the men wore strings of coral beads on their necks. Some of them wore more than one.

Their garments were ankle-length, flowing with different motifs. These garments were worn over wide matching breeches and some over wraparounds that resemble the women's. The motifs on these garments were lion's head, tiger's head, dog's head, and elephant's head.

I noticed one of the men whose attire appeared distinctively different from the others. He wore a large loose robe of satin lace, richly trimmed and embroidered with intricate patterns of contrasting colors. He bunched this robe at the shoulders.

His necklaces were strings of cowry shells and orange-colored, cylinder-like beads. His staff was of dazzling brass. He also wore a crown-like hat made of a combination of gold and red velvet. He was also holding a leather fan edged with ostrich plumes and a whisk which looked more like the tail of a horse. His footwear was a pair of highly designed sandals.

He walked gracefully in, accompanied by a gorgeously dressed woman who seemed to be his wife. All the men he met on his way greeted him in a very special way -- beating their fans against his three times to the side and then concluding with a stroke at the middle. Those that were not holding fans simulated with their bare hands. He finally sat down among the rest of the people.

The women came in what appeared to be their traditional wraparound fashion. Each of which appeared to portray certain knowledge of each individual's impeccable taste. The wraparounds were long draped cloths, which extended from the waist to the heels.

Most of the women were rather loaded than adorned with gold necklaces, pendants and bracelets. One could not help but hear the rustling of clothes and the ringing, chiming and clanking of accumulation of metal bangles. The children's outfits were not as sophisticated and complicated as those of the adults. They wore the traditional sleeveless tunics, trousers and hats some of which matched and some of which did not match.

The Ceremony

The hall inside was equally decorated with some motifs and artifacts. These artifacts appeared to transmit some type of information about the people or the occasion. The chairs and tables were arranged in the corners and sides of the hall, leaving a large open space in the center.

The hall was packed full by 9:30 p.m. A gentleman who appeared to be the Master of Ceremonies stood by the microphone and greeted the crowd, quieting the loud exchanges that sounded like a flock of humming birds in flight. He then announced the name of someone whom he said would administer the rituals for the evening. The crowd cheered as he stood.

It was the same man that had caught my eyes earlier. He walked to the special table reserved for him at one end of the hall directly facing the open space.

His wife accompanied him to the table. Her headpiece was a bulky, untailored rectangles of cloth (or so it appeared), which matched the color of her laced blouse. From the back, I could see her hair woven into beautiful tresses.

A few other elders were called to sit with the "Ritual lord." When the applause subsided, he stood to speak. He spoke in the native dialect: He cleared his throat as if to call the people's attention to him.

Ndi eze, Kelenu!
The chiefs, I greet you

Ndi ozo, Kelenu!
Titled men, I greet you

Umu Igbo, Kwenu!
The Igbo, I salute you

Ihe anyi biara ime bu omenala
We are here to perform our custom.

Onye o bula gee nti nke oma
Listen very attentively

Ka m kpokuo ndi ichie____
I'll call on the ancestors____

The ancestors are our source of strength and power, and we must call upon them first before doing anything else.

Our life will not be complete without them.

They are our responsibility. We want to re-establish and re-emphasize our belief.

We want to communicate with them, and to do so requires that we give our undivided attention.

This is not entertainment. It is a serious business. It is our religion, our way of life. We want to leave the material and seek the spiritual. We want to solicit the guidance and protection of the gods of the land.

The Transcending Ladder

After these words, he was silent. This silence seemed to be contagious. The audience silenced with him.

His silence at this point seemed to convey a serene sense of spiritual transcendence. He looked blankly at the crowd---looking at them, but seeing something else.

His posture evoked the image of one who listens attentively to the messages of a higher order. It was the type of silence, which transforms everyday objects into mute symbols in an attempt to get at the occult voices of heaven. It was the type that opens up the empty twilight zone of one's own familiar interior.

It was a moment of transcendence, an attempt to capture a high spiritual elevation, a state in which the spirit suppresses all verbal expression and becomes a fertile ground for the advent of the superhuman.

It was stillness eloquent of something. He seemed to be experiencing a new life on a superhuman plane, which lied beyond the realm of language. He appeared to be cultivating silence in order to evoke the image of the ancestors who dwell below in silence, to listen to their profound secrets, the secrets of man's innermost being.

The silence was an ascending ladder, which connected the material world with the spiritual, giving the soul the inevitable extension and transcendence and carrying it to the realm of pure light.

When he began again to speak. He called once again on the ancestors:

Ndi Ichie   Our Ancestors

He began softly, as if attempting to induce a strong mystic and linguistic isolation. He was in a state of silent listening in which he felt closest to the secrets of the invisible realm.

It was in this type of silence that spiritual voices become clear, and it was this silent clarity, attentive to those forces hidden beneath the surface of the common-place that the Chief Ritualist appeared to seek, a spiritual solitude, so captivating, so intimate, so consummating, so profound, so personal.

The silent images were so strong and appeared to induce a struggle between the body and the imagination. He seemed to be undertaking a journey to the world of the psyche, attempting to make the invisible visible, creating a combination of complex and ambiguous images.

Ndi nnanna anyi ha
Our forefathers
Ala Igbo
The land of the Igbo

Ala America
The land of America

He recognized the land that they were presently on (the land of America),
signifying that "Ala" ("Mother Earth") is the same all over the world.

Ndewonu!
I salute you!

Ebe anyi siri bia di anya,
Our home is far away,

Kama, Chi anyi na-edu anyi.
But, our God is our guide.

He pointed upward to the sky when he mentioned God, thus signifying
their belief in God as the Almighty who dwells in heaven.

O biara nga onye abiagbula ya.
Let the visitor not bring death to host.

Ya lawa, nkpunkpu apula ya.
And when he leaves, do so in peace.

Egbe bere; Ugo bere
Let the kite perch, let the eagle perch also.

His tone of voice was consistent all through. He appeared to be in a state
of melancholy, of ominous splendor, of breathless, empty stillness. He seemed to
feel the presence of those he was talking to. The audience's participation during
the monologue was minimal.

Igbo, mmammanu!
The Igbo, I salute you

His tone of voice rose at this time. His face seemed to unfold. He seemed to have come back to normal state of being.

Igbo, Kelenu!
The Igbo, I greet you
Igbo, nuonu!
The Igbo, drink for health!
Igbo, rienu!
The Igbo, eat for health!

He sat down and began to fan himself. A cheery murmur swept the crowd.

The announcer took the microphone again and called on one of the cultural groups to present its dance. At that moment, the "Ritual lord" interrupted ---

No! No! No! No! No!
We must first break kolanut.

Kolanut is a symbol of welcome, and it must be administered first as an exchange of goodwill. The "Ritual lord" began to speak again. This time, he spoke the English language:

This is the most important aspect of our being, and, of course, the most important aspect of this occasion. We are about to go to the spirit house, and we ask that our visitors who may not understand to please bear with us. I will now go back to the native tongue, because the ritual that I am about to perform cannot be done in a foreign language.

Before he began to speak again, he cleared his throat. Throat clearing seemed to precede every call to libation and ancestral solicitation.

He seemed to clear his throat to acquire the voice different from one in ordinary human conversation. Perhaps it caused the spirits to listen or called the attention of the mortal to the presence of the immortal.

Igbo, Kwenu!
Igbo, Kwenu!
Bende, Kwenu!
Kwezuenu!

After each greeting the crowd responded with a resounding, "Yaah!" He held up a plate full of kolanut.

Oji Igbo anaghi aga njem.
Kolanut in Igboland doesn't travel.

Ewerela m oji a zi nde Umuahia.
I've shown the kolanut to the Umuahia community.

Ewerela m oji a zi nde Ikwuano.
I've shown the kolanut to the Ikwuano community.

Nkpa, Nkporo, Abiriba,
Abam, Umuhu, Ututu, Arochukwu, Ihechiowa, Umunnato, Alayi,
Item, Ozuitem, Igbere.

He walked to the center of the hall, held up one of the kolanuts. Silence.

Ndi ichie Bende, unu were oji.
Bende Ancestors, here's kolanut.

Ndi ichie Igbo, Unu were oji.
Igbo ancestors, here's kolanut.

Ndi ichie Nigeria, unu were oji.
Ancestors of Nigeria, here's kolanut.

Ndi ichie Africa, unu were oji.
Ancestor of Africa, here's kolanut.

174

Onye choro ihe oma, ihe oma biara ya.
Grant peace to the peacemaker.

Ndu ogolologo.
Long life.

Omumu.
Offsprings.

Aku na uba.
Prosperity.

Udo na onu.
Peace and joy.

He broke the kolanut and tossed the pieces on the floor. Then he said:

     I have given the ancestors their share. When the kolanuts is given to *Ala* (Mother Earth), it has reached the ancestors who were taken by Mother Earth into her bossom.
     The ancestors are satisfied. I'm satisfied. It is our duty to do so, and it has been done.

He walked back to his seat. The crowd was dead silent. He picked up a bottle of wine or some type of drink in a bottle and returned to the center floor. He began to speak again:

     Our ancestors cannot take half measures. We have given them kolanut. We must also give them drink. I must complete this ceremony so that when I go home tonight, I can sleep well in my bed.

Ndi ichie Bende.
The ancestors of Bende.

Ndi ichie Igbo
The ancestors of Igbo.

Ndi ichie Nigeria
The ancestors of Nigeria.

Ndi ichie Africa
The ancestors of Africa.

Unu lee mmanya.
This wine is for you.

He poured some of the contents of the bottle on the floor three times and walked back to his seat. The audience watched in rapt attention.

The "Ritual lord" appeared to be playing the role of a mediator, a bridge between two worlds---the world of the ancestors and the world of humans. His voice all through the ritual was reverent, and he appeared to be emotionally charged and spirit-filled. The hall was replete with silence all through the monologue, and their participation continued to be minimal.

This ritual was a means of communication. It was performed to solicit the guidance and protection of the gods of the land. The audience's silence was equivocal of something spiritual---a concentration upon the unseen and the unheard. It suggested a mysterious reality beyond appearance.

This ritual drama appeared to be symbolic of the struggle of the mortal being against exterior forces. It was an attempt to tap the vital energy that controls life, an attempt to make the invisible visible and the intangible tangible.

The Ritual Lord reassured the audience and invited them to partake of the food. His voice was strong and confident:

Now, everyone can eat the kolanut and drink. We have pleased our ancestors, and we know that they will in turn please us. This time, we are going to experience the best. We are waiting for the arrival of our ancestors from the spirit world. Please, mothers, hold your children. Okonko is coming!

The Okonko was coming from the spirit world. It was coming to reassure the people. It was the visible manifestation of the invisible---the dead fathers, the ancestors. The *Okonko* was a means of reuniting with the fathers from the underworld.

Soon, the drummers came in. They were all men, five in all, each playing a different instrument. They were dressed in traditional costumes. Music went to fever pitch.

The dancers came in, all women, dressed uniquely---draped cloth around their waists and across their chests, leaving the stomach and the shoulders bare. The leggings on their ankles shook and rattled as they danced. The white handkerchiefs in their hands flung back and forth in ecstatic frenzy.

As they danced, people threw money on their faces. When the money was thrown, they always allowed it to touch the ground before it was picked up, not by the dancer, usually, but by someone else who was perhaps designated to do so.

Throwing money on dancers signified more than a show of wealth because even the less fortunate threw_money. It was a sign that the dancer was doing a good job.

More than these, it was a symbol of goodwill and continuity. When the money touched the ground, it was believed to have touched the source of all wealth. It was the receiver's way of asking the "Giver of Wealth" to prosper and multiply the giver.

Meanwhile, women placed food on people's tables. Each plate of food consists of rice, *mahi-mahi*, baked chicken roasted goat meat and *suya*.

The drummers and the dancers performed for approximately fifteen minutes. It was over. The dancers left first. After a little time of playing, the drummers stopped and left. The audience applauded.

The "Ritual lord" stood again, cleared his throat and called for silence. Everyone was quiet. He began to speak:

177

Before we eat, our forefathers must eat. This way we will be sure that the food will give us health and not sickness. I see that everyone has some food on the table. Once again, I must do this for our health.

He picked up a plate of food, muttered some unintelligible incantations, waved the plate on the air three times, in silence, placed it down on the table and began to speak again.

Our ancestors live in our memories and in the family ritual in which they receive offerings of food and drinks. When we give our ancestors before we eat, we honor them, and they, in turn, honor us by giving us protection and abundance of life. We can now eat and drink.

He sat down, shook hands with the other elders who stood up as if to affirm. Meanwhile, the disc jockey had begun to play some music, first on low volume as the elders shook hands, then he turned it high as people began to eat. It was a free time, so to speak.

People walked around greeting others, perhaps those that they didn't have the chance to greet earlier or those they just saw for the first time. Others ate, and others sat and talked. The eating and drinking lasted for about thirty minutes.

The Igbo are very effervescent, gregarious and vivacious, very ebullient, extroverted and loquacious, especially in their greetings and interactions. They interact openly with complete strangers. Greeting is boisterous and generously exchanged.

No matter how many times one crosses the other greetings are exchanged. These greetings come in different forms---hugging, screaming, clapping, and jumping. It is against this background of boisterous and loquacious vivacity that their silence could be understood.

Okonko

The music stopped. The "Ritual lord" picked up the microphone, stood up, cleared his throat and said:

> The time we have been waiting for has come. This is the time to reunite with our ancestors from the spirit world. For the interest of our visitors and our children who are not aware, Okonko is among the most important masquerades of the Igbo.

Okonko masquerades are the manifestations of the spirits. They are the ancestors, the dead fathers of the clan who appear to the people in these forms. They are the visitors from the land of the dead.

Membership into the Okonko society is reserved for men of honor and integrity. It consists of six drums: *Oke nkwa, Nne nkwa, Ada nkwa, Oso nkwa, Awa nkwa Odozi nkwa, and Ogene.*

These drums are a symbol of family. *Oke nkwa* (Male drum) signifies Father, *Nne nkwa* (Female drum) signifies Mother, *Ada nkwa* (First female drum) signifies Daughter, *Oso nkwa* (second drum) signifies a second child (boy or girl) in the family, while *Awa nkwa* and *Odozi nkwa* signify the coordination of the whole community.

Ogene (metal gong) is the town crier's instrument used to send messages to all the community. It is used here also as a symbol of communication between the two worlds---the material world and the spiritual world.

Okonko is played during the New Yam festival to give thanks to the Mother Earth and the gods for fruitful harvest. It is played during funeral to pay respect to a departing elder. During these ceremonies, Okonko appeared to reassure the people.

One could sense the heightened anticipation in the eyes of the people. Even the elders seemed anxious. Those who were sitting behind taller people stood up, peering toward the anticipated direction from which the okonko would emerge.

A bell rang from a distance, then closer, closer, and closer, then it became sonorous. All was silent. In the midst of so much crowd, one could hear a pin drop. A man dressed in short, red, green and white striped skirt walked in, holding a bell in one hand and a rattle metal in the other. A line of white chalk ran across his eyes. His chest, arms, legs were all painted with white chalk. The rattles in his ankles shook to his solid, steady steps.

He walked straight to the table where the elders and the Ritual lord were sitting, stopped, struck his metal rattle once on the floor, rang the bell one more time, adjusted the yellow ostrich feather on his red cap, turned around, shook his bare chest and walked his way back to where he had come from.

Visitors from Underworld

Moments later, the drums began to beat. First it was distant, then close, then closer. Six drummers came in, already perspiring. It seemed like they had been playing for hours in the sun. They were all dressed like the herald. They walked to a corner of the open space, sat down on the chairs provided for them and continued. People cheered, but their eyes were still gazing at the entrance.

A horn sounded, piercing through the music. Two young children came in, dancing to the beat of the intricate rhythm of the drums. The lead drummer's hands began to move rapidly, raising the music to fever pitch. Soon shouts emanated within the dressing room. The bell rang, again and again. First, a group of men came in chanting and dancing.

Soon, the Okonko appeared, jumping and stomping with the agility of a leopard, the strength of a tiger, the majesty of a lion and the elasticity of a cat. Seconds later, another Okonko followed, then another and another. The hall broke apart. People cheered and screamed.

The appearance of the Okonko was a spectacular sight. The colorful rustling costumes, the awe-inspiring mask, the dangling bells, and the chiming, the ringing and the clanking that accentuated the gestures of its movement.

180

The masquerades appeared to satisfy the Igbo artistic appetite very much. They were an embodiment of their arts: sculpture, music, painting, drama, and even architecture, and they involved different and diverse theatrical elements such as masks and costumes, movement and dance, music and song, mime, and character.

The Okonko swirled and stamped. The rattles and bells on their waists shook in ecstatic frenzy. People surged forward as if to behold the dancing visitors from the underworld.

The elders stood up and joined them. The Ritual lord waved his staff in the air in jubilation. He danced to the drummers, threw money on them, danced to the Okonko and threw money on them one by one. The elders followed. Others in the crowd who wished to throw money came out, dancing and spraying money. It was a total celebration.

The masquerades defied gravity as they swirled and stumped. They seemed to be possessed. They spoke in esoteric voices.

The audience responded differently. The masquerades seemed to have brought with them a range of feelings that affect the audience totally, from moments of psychic shock, of terror, of mortal danger, to moments of fascination, of inspiration and admiration.

The drums continued to beat, the flutes continued to sing, and the spectators continued to cheer and watch in transfixed mixture of awe and admiration.

The masquerades danced non-stop for the entire half hour. They executed and maintained their footwork with such consummate vitality and their bodies with such percussive explosion of strength, stamping, stomping, tumbling, swirling, rolling, and jumping, exhibiting such intensive kinetic flair, such speed, such agility, such elasticity with such rhythmic impulse.

For someone to dance that long with such unstoppable agility, there must have been some strength and energy flowing from somewhere. The masks appeared all the more rigid in the midst of the violent and relentless movements of the dance.

The faces of the masks were awe-inspiring, causing some of the women present to seek cover behind the men. Some of them had bulged eyes, big geometric noses that stretched from the eyes to the upper lips. Some of their tongues stuck out from the corners of their mouths.

Gouges of facial marks crises-crossed their cheeks. They resembled nothing that any mortal has seen or will ever see in real life, in a dream, maybe.

Three of the masks had closed eyes and mouths, but their dynamic momentum was not completely silenced. They appeared to contain some vital energy, a natural force, which gave them a particular artistic suggestive power.

One of the masquerades ran into the audience perhaps to scare or intimidate people. It flung its whip against tables and walls, jumping and swinging. The women and some men in the area fled in silent confusion, but there wasn't anywhere to run but to fall on each other, causing a huge stampede.

As soon as it made its way back to the dancing arena, somebody threw a cold raw egg on the face of the mask which splattered all over the place, even on people's clothes. At that moment, the masquerade slowed down.

Moments later, it left. It was the first masquerade to depart the arena. This mask was dark-faced and seemed to express some qualities of ugliness and fierceness. It had two pierced eyes and gaping teeth.

The pieced eyes seemed to reflect or express some inner agitation, some intrinsic unrest. It appeared to depict a wandering ghost, perhaps the ghost of one of the fathers who departed in a foreign land and thus, had not reached its proper resting place. It was probably frustrated and venting its anger on the people.

This would seem to contradict the initial interpretation of the universality of Mother Earth. However, it would be safe to conclude that the proper resting place for a departed Igbo would be Igboland.

The presentation of this type of mask in this ceremony was not totally surprising since there were some Igbo who had died in the United States, but whose bodies, for some reason, did not make it home.

It was this type of spirit that was placated during rituals so as to keep their aggression in check. It would be safe to conclude then that the ancestral spirit and the mask form a single entity such that one cannot be dissociated from the other.

In carving his mask, the artist attempts to depict this phenomenon. He breathes silent heat and energy into the masks as he carves, and it is this silent heat, this silent roar, this silent pulse that ruptures into a percussive vitality during performance.

Meanwhile, the drummers took the arena for few more minutes. This time, the women came to dance and throw money on the drummers. Soon, the drummers stood and drummed away. The people applauded.

The "Ritual lord" thanked everyone for coming, and declared the event over. People began to disperse. It was about 5:25 a.m.

Conclusion

During such masquerade performances, when the drums begin to beat those nostalgic rhythms, the dancers are possessed. During the time of possession, they are no longer themselves. The spirit takes complete control. New energy comes into the person-spirit such that even an old person who ordinarily wobbles begins to stomp, stamp, tumble, swirl, roll_and jump.

Their appearances change. Their faces glow; their eyes bulge, and the pupils roll to an uncanny glitter. The faces freeze and the cheeks expand with balloon-like elasticity. Sometimes they gape their teeth or thrust out their tongues.

The audience appears pleased because the people see the ancestors, the forefathers and founders of their lineage reuniting with them in these forms. The masquerades do not represent the beings from the underworld; they are such beings. They are not human beings hiding behind a mask for trick or treat; they are spirits. They embody the reincarnated spirits of the ancestors. Once the soul of the ancestor possesses the soul of the wearer, he explodes with a rupture of energy and undiminished stamina, transcending the pathos of mortality.

The mask of Africa, like their beliefs and customs, is the product of an age of faith. "For men directly involved in procuring the means of subsistence, whether by hunting or cultivating, some control over the environment is in urgent need" (Graham-White, 1974, p. 15); hence Africans regard their masks as a means of controlling the environment and harnessing the power of their ancestors and the supernatural forces.

In sculpture, in dance, in music, Africans attempt to express and celebrate the moral and religious convictions that underlay their daily life (Davidson, 1971). Their artists are therefore concerned mainly with the spiritual content of their work.

Traditional African masquerading is still staged today despite the overwhelming influx of foreign influences. This is partly because African art is a part of the daily life of the people, and as Ogunba (1978) adds, it is "woven around diverse beings and physical phenomena ranging from powerful gods and goddesses to hill and water spirits and the generality of illustrious ancestors" (p.3).

Moreover, their gods and spirits are still walking and talking. They are still very powerful and have continued to thrive regardless of the pressure from alien civilization and culture.

Nothing in this volume suggests a detailed uniqueness of the African world. However, an attempt has been made to explore and examine, in perspective, the cultural traits of this wondrous world as they influence their art and their life in a distant land.

Finally, it is essential to point out that all cultures have rituals which they identify with and which they are identified by. It is equally possible that other cultures have similar rituals and perspectives as discussed in this paper. Researchers are encouraged, therefore, to seek out and examine those rituals and perspectives.

CHAPTER 13

"Through a Glass Dimly"

POWER

Traditional/Normative Power:

    The power mostly exhibited during these festivals was the normative power. The Chief Ritualist appeared to possess this power which stemmed in part from his status as the Chief Ritualist and his role as the Chief Priest, the mortal intercessor, and from the people's tacit awareness of the existence of spirits and the world beyond, their religious inclination, their knowledge of the Supernatural and their unalloyed respect and acceptance of the Chief Ritualist's role in the community.

    This power was cultural; hence internal to the people's volition. There was consent in the part of the audience, cringing humility, again based on the knowledge and acceptance of the norm, the belief, the culture, the tradition. He commanded the people's loyalty because they trusted him and believed in him. People were hungry, but they did not start eating until he asked them to: "We can now eat and drink." "Now everyone can eat the kolanuts and drink."

Supernatural/Divine Power:

    This power was internalized. It seemed to embrace all mystery. It was an infinitely complex idea. Everyone was aware of the magnitude of this power. It was this tacit awareness that was reflected in the traditional power invested in the Chief Ritualist.

ROLES

A. The Chief Ritualist:

(1) <u>The Chief Priest</u>: He was the Chief Priest, a religious leader who served as the intercessor between the gods, the spirits, the ancestors and the people, the community, the tribe.

(2) <u>A bridge between two worlds</u>: He was a bridge between two worlds--- the mortal world and the spiritual world. He received the messages of the higher order, in silence, just like the biblical prophets of the Old Testament. He knew when the time was right to eat, when the gods had given their okay, then he communicated thus to the people.

(3) <u>A traditional father</u>: He sat at the head of the table and led the offerings. He was in closest proximity with the spiritual forces and knew how to tap the vital energy.

B. The Earth goddess (Mother Earth):

(1) <u>A kind mother</u>: She welcomes her children and receives them in her bosom.

(2) <u>A caring mother</u>: She nurtures and protects her children.

(3) <u>A loving mother</u>: She provides food for her children---gives fertility to crops and to human beings.

(4) <u>A judge:</u> She is the ultimate judge of morality and conduct.

C. Masquerades:

(1) <u>A Nodal point</u>: Masquerade is a nodal point in African culture. Nodal points are points at which important strands of culture intersect. Masquerades subsume all forms of the art---painting, sculpture (masks), costumes, drama, dance, music, movement, mime, and even architecture.

(2) <u>A Religious symbol</u>: Masquerades represent a very important aspect of African religion. Their role is to reaffirm, at regular intervals, the truth and the immediate presence of myths in everyday life.

186

(3) An abode for a spirit: "The masquerader is not a man pretending to be a god. He is god in its absolute sense. Everybody obeys him, and no requests may be denied him.

(4) A communication medium: Masquerade is a means of expressing the inexpressible. It is a source of communication with the ancestors and the gods of the land. It serves as an instrument by which contacts are made with the supernatural forces.

(5) The judiciary: Passes judgment during judicial proceedings and settles disputes.

(6) Police/Executive agent: Punishes every breech of the custom.

(7) The intercessor: It intercedes on behalf of the people during planting season to ensure fecundity, to send rain in times of severe drought.
Whenever there is danger and the lurking of evil sorcerers who cannot be dealt with by material means, the masks and masquerades intercede.

(8) The guardian spirit: During funerals and when the souls of the dead are driven so that they may set out on their journey to the spirit world, masks come to play, to ensure easy transition, from material to spiritual.

D. Ancestors:
    (1) The source of life and prosperity.
    (2) The fixed point of reference
    (3) The fathers of the land.

BINARY OPPOSITIONS
(1)   Power: Traditional/Normative Vs Spiritual/Divine
(2)   Heaven Vs Earth
(3)   Male Vs Female
(4)   Spiritual world Vs Material world
(5)   Silence Vs Loquacity
(6)   Benevolent Spirit Vs Malevolent Spirit

(7)   Old age Vs Youth

(8)   Spirit-regarding Vs Man-regarding

1. Power: Traditional/Normative vs. Spiritual/Divine

Traditional power among the Africans is wielded by the male authority figure. This power stems in part from his status as a father, the head of the household, from his position and role in the community, and from the people's tacit awareness and acceptance of his person, and their respect for his authority.

This power is cultural; hence internal to the people's volition. He must command the people's loyalty because they must trust him and believe in him.

It is internalized, and everyone is aware of its magnitude. It embraces all mystery, and it is manifested in their tacit awareness of the existence of the Almighty God, the spirits, and the world beyond.

It is reflected in the power invested on their religious priests who is the mortal intercessor. Everyone seems to be in awe of this power because of the seemingly human's lack of control over it.

2.   Heaven vs. Earth

Africans conceive of heaven as the dwelling place for the Almighty God. Among the Igbo, for example, heaven is believed to be the abode of *Chukwu Abiama* (God Almighty), maker of all things. They see Him as His name indicates---*Chi Ukwu* (A Big God), the Supreme Being, *Chineke* ("*Chi na Eke*"), which means God and Creation.

Their world revolves completely around this God that they give names such as *Chika* (God is Supreme), *Kelechi* (Give Thanks to God), *Chidinma* (God is Good), *Onyinyechi* (The gift of God), *Chijindu* (God, the Author of Life), *Chizuruoke* (God is Perfect). Because they do not see this God who is in heaven, the Igbo create works of art as "aids to devotion," the same as the artworks or statues found in other religions and in some Christian churches.

188

Earth is the abode of Mother Earth (*Ala*) the overseer of all supreme reproductions. *Ala* is a kind mother who welcomes all her children and receives them in her bosom.

She does not discriminate against anybody. She welcomes the murderer just the same. She is a caring mother who nurtures and protects her children, and a loving mother who provides food for all, gives fertility to crops and to her children.

She is the ultimate judge of morality and conduct. She is patient and does not kill for minor offences, but she strikes immediately and without hesitation when one purposely desecrates the land and fails to propitiate the earth.

3.   Male Vs Female

The male in Africa is an institution. To be a male carries with it some aura of spirituality beyond masculinity. Women who could not bear sons for their husbands are said to have not fulfilled their obligations in a marriage. This is one of the reasons men marry more than one wife in Africa, in "search" for a son, an heir. Sometimes, it is a reasonable ground for a divorce.

Only the men perform rituals during cultural festivals. When an animal is slaughtered, some parts of it are reserved specifically for the men. The head also belongs to the son of the house. The head is the seat of life, and men are said to be the head of the family or household. They are supposed to be in closest proximity with the gods of the land. Women are forbidden to eat the foods used for sacrifice. The ancestors whose protection and guidance are sought during planting season, war, fishing and hunting expeditions are all men---the dead fathers of the clan.

In Africa, a person's destiny is determined in the beginning of the person's life, and one does not live beyond and above his destiny. To make certain that one's destiny remains good through life, the Africans, for instance the Igbo, use a carved figure called "Ikenga" which represents the power of a man's right hand.

It is when the man's life is good that the woman's life becomes good. The man, the head of the family, is like the actual human head. When it is cut off, the other parts of the body die. In Africa, the woman is regarded as a part of the man. This concept probably takes root from the biblical account of the creation of Eve (from Adam's ribs).

African mask carvers are all men. It is not so because of their dexterity, masculinity, or talent, but mainly because of their spiritual relationship with those whose images are being carved in the masks and figures and whose spirits are being evoked with those images.

4.   Spiritual World Vs Material World

African worldview is primarily religious. They realize that there is a cosmic rhythm operating on different levels other than their own. They, therefore, solicit the powers of the spirits, the vital energy, to help them deal with material matters, to deal with life and fortunes.

Spirits are solicited during planting season, hunting and fishing expeditions and war. They are solicited for good health, for wealth, for fecundity. The carved masks and figures are used during such rituals to represent the world of the spirits (the immortal) while man himself represents the material (the mortal).

The intensive and vigorous theatrical performances of the spirits of the ancestors (the masquerades from the spirit world) are caught and expressed in the magical formulas of art in mask carving which comprises an intricate set of man's activities in the material world. The rituals performed are an attempt to tap the life force from the spiritual realm which controls life in the material world, and during these rituals, the Africans cultivate silence as a means of escaping the material world in order to attain spiritual elevation, to transcend the pathos of mortality.

5. Silence Vs Loquacity

Africans are very extroverted in all their everyday activities. Among the Igbo, for example, greetings are boisterously and extravagantly exchanged. They cheer, applaud, scream, clap and jump. When they dance, they exhibit such energy-filled stamina, such kinetic flair, such exuberance, stomping and stamping, spinning and swirling, rocking and pivoting with agility, strength and elasticity. They maintain their footwork with such percussive animism, causing their rattles to shake and agitate in ecstatic frenzy.

Discussions are loud and long. Their exuberance and effervescence are even manifested in the rustling of their costumes, the dangling of their pendants, necklaces and earrings, the chiming and clanking of the wristlets and anklets as they walk.

This people use lots of loud instruments---the horns that pierce through the tight air, the drums that beat and beat and beat, raising music to fever pitch, the bells that ring again and again and again to a sonorous tintinnabulation, signaling the arrival of the visitors from the land of the dead.

Above this ebullient background of effervescence, exuberance and loquacity hovers such a mysterious thick, dark cloud of silence that descends at intervals like a heavy thunderstorm and floods their world with absolute somnolence and taciturnity. During rituals, the whole place is replete with silence, conjuring images that are so complex, yet so vivid and capable of catapulting one into a world where silent voices whisper peace, assurance, life, health, prosperity. During funerals, silence becomes the eloquence of the unspoken.

6. Benevolent Vs Malevolent

African mask performs the function of liberating the actor into the character. It deals with the relation of man to those supernatural, divine powers which are sometimes felt to be irrational, sometimes cruel, and sometimes just, and reveals, in one way or another, man's belief in his nature and destiny and the nature of the world in which he lives.

There are the spirits of the souls of the ancestors, which were not properly laid to rest or the wandering spirits let loose in a foreign land, which lurk, looking for who to devour. Such spirits are kept in check by soliciting the powers of the good spirits through sacrifices.

During mask carving, trees are cut down. These trees are inhabited by spirits, thus, when the trees are felled, such spirits are rendered homeless, and could be malicious. To placate them, sacrifices are offered. If they continue to be malevolent, more powerful spirits are evoked to keep them in check.

Masked dancers wear long costumes to protect them from the dangerous spell of the wandering spirits. When a person dies, certain energy is released. If left unchecked, this could cause disaster to the community.

7.   **Old Age Vs Youth**

In Africa, only the oldest in the family or community offers libations during rituals and sacrifices. Old age is an institution. The old are said to be in closest contact with the dead and Mother Earth. They are venerated and adored.

They are the lucky ones who have survived the ills of the mortal world and are able to attain the age of wisdom. The ultimate goal of an African youth is to attain the age of wisdom and be in a position to lead the family and community into the spiritual realm.

8.   **Spirit-Regarding Vs Man-Regarding**

African world is an arena for interplay of forces (Achebe, 1984). The Africans believe in the existence of spirits, and they attempt to please all the gods at all times. They also believe in a Supreme Being whom they perceive as directly unapproachable; hence they device a means of reaching Him. It is this belief system that brings African art into existence.

192

Among the Igbo of Africa which is essentially a chiefless tribe, there is no central authority, as could be found among the Yoruba and Benin. Means of living is by tapping the ancestors through works of art.

Communication is through prayer, sacrifice, music and dance, and their art plays a very important role in this worship and interaction. It is this striving to come in terms with a multitude of forces that gives Igbo life its tense and restless dynamism. It is this concept of spiritual forces that makes their art spirit-regarding.

Man-regarding art (art made to honor man) is materialistically embellished to portray the power, wealth and grandeur of the monarch or the patron. It gears more toward naturalism and realism. Some of the Baroque and Renaissance portrait paintings and sculptures could be classified in this category.

Igbo art, made to tap vital energy, the life force, is made to resemble nothing known or seen by man. By consciously distorting proportions, the artist achieves the concept of the ancestor or spirit. The vitality of the carved images stem from sacrifices; hence masks and figures which span generations are regarded as exceptionally powerful.

Conclusion

Ka ohia di ka enwe amaghi ya. Ubochi nta, k'anyi chuo na owere nchi. K'anyi na-eti aku, ka oka anyi na-agba tom tom n'oku. Egbe bere; Ugo bere. O biara nga onye abiagbula ya; ya lawa nkpunkpu apula ya. O chu nwa okuko nwe ada; nwa okuko nwe ngwengwe oso.

As we break kolanut and pour our libations, we seal the faith that cultural understanding will someday join people together, because when people are joined together, the world is joined together. Let the Kite perch; let the Egret perch.

Questions, Discussions, and Activities

NEW YAM FESTIVAL

1.   In Onny's culture, they celebrate the **New Yam Festival**. New Yam Festival was a time to celebrate the first fruits of the harvest. It was a time for families to come together and give thanks for fecundity, life, and health.

Discuss some of the activities that take place during the New Yam Festival in Onny's culture. Can you identify a similar celebration in your own culture? What are some of the similarities and differences?

RITES OF PASSAGE

2.   Different cultures perform different rituals to celebrate passage from childhood to adulthood

Can you identify and discuss such ritual in Onny's culture? Work in groups to research and document details about rites of passage among any culture of your choice. Have each group discuss their findings and then make a table showing similarities and differences.

SCHOOL AND SCHOOLING

3.   Education system varies from culture to culture.
Describe the education system in Onny's culture. What are the roles of the teachers and the students? What types of discipline strategies are used in the schools? What type of instructional strategy did Onny's teacher apply in the English lesson? Compare the system of education in Onny's culture with your own educational system.

HOME REMEDIES

4.   In Onny's culture "Dogoyaro" was one of the cure-all prescriptions for all maladies.

What are the other types of home remedies used by the people of this culture? Can you think of any home remedy used in your culture? Do you find any similarities?

FAMILY VALUES

Familism

Familism is the emphasis on the importance of family. There is an important belief in family in Onny's culture. Family unit is very strong and sacred, and it includes grandparents, uncles, aunts, cousins, and other distant relatives. The family is considered important over the individual; hence the needs of the individual are subordinated to those of the family.

Describe the characteristics of your family. Construct a Genogram (Family Tree) that reflects your family relationships and family responsibility.

Filial Piety

Filial piety is the respect for parents. Children are taught to respect their parents, grandparents in Onny's culture. In many cultures of the world, respect for parents is considered a strong family value.

Discuss ways in which your culture shows respect to their parents and elders. How has the transition affected this African immigrant family value?

Respect for the Elderly

Old age is an institution, and children are taught to care for their parents in their old age. Children in Onny's culture are taught to respect their elders. This includes all elderly persons whether the person is a member of the family or not. The same respect giving to the living older family member is also accorded to the dead (the ancestors).

Identify how respect is accorded to the dead in Onny's culture. Can you identify any other cultures where similar values and practices could be found?

Respect for Authority

In Onny's culture, respect for authority is emphasized in the family. This core family value is displayed both at home and at school. Children respect their teachers and hold them in a very high esteem. They are looked upon as the authority figures.

How do students in Onny's culture display respect for their teachers? How is respect for authority displayed in your culture among parents and teachers?

Food

In Onny's culture, *foo-foo* is the staple food eaten by all. It is made with specially prepared cassava, which is rolled into small balls and dipped in soup. *Foo-foo* is eaten with fingers.

Can you identify other foods eaten in Onny's culture? What is the staple food of your culture? Do you eat with your hands? If not, what do you eat with? Can you identify other cultures that have finger foods? What other materials do people of other cultures eat with?

Food Taboos
Certain foods are forbidden in Onny's culture. Children are taught early to avoid foods that are considered sacred or detrimental to health. Such foods may include certain mushrooms, meat, fish, snails, etc

What is the common food taboo in your culture? Do you know any other foods that are considered taboos in other cultures?

Chores
Children in Onny's culture help their parents at home. They also help their parents with their farm work. Onny would gather firewood and tie them up for sale. He would help his father stake the yams and mend the fences. In different cultures, children do different things to help out their parents.

What do children do to help their parents at home in your culture? Make a list of the chores you do at home and compare them with the chores Onny would do. Do you know of any culture in which children do different kinds of chores?

The Art Experience

Using a model for art criticism, lead the students to a discussion of masks, analyzing, interpreting and evaluating, given the cultural contexts already discussed. Then have the students create a mask of their choice.

You should encourage the students to create masks that express something from their own culture as the African mask carvers express something from their culture. This is necessary because this whole concept of multi-cultural and cross-cultural art experience, as far as this study is concerned, is not to reproduce or copy the mask of Africa; it is to make African mask meaningful in the lives of the students.

You will decide the materials to be used. Small size boxes, construction papers and paper bags could be used to fashion the masks while the students' imaginations are allowed to go riot with beads, strings, yarns, pebbles, and other found objects.

The students could break boundaries, invent or push boundaries. After the mask is completed, the teacher could have the students form "masquerade groups", bring old sheets or costumes from home or elsewhere, and enact masquerade performances. Have each group discuss its experience(s) and say which function(s) the masquerade was meant to perform and so on.

This provides a wonderful opportunity for cohesive learning that can be sparked as teachers work together with this cultural phenomenon of the mask. An English teacher could have the students write about masks from the experience of being the character that the mask conveys on them. It could also be seen working in History classes---the kinds of masks that these cultures wear, what the cultures were that these masks are from and exploring those cultures in Social Studies.

Just have fun. Good luck!

References

Achebe, C. (1984). Art of the Igbo world. In H. M. Cole & C. C. Aniakor. Igbo arts, community and cosmos. Los Angeles: University of California Press.

Achebe, C. (1959). *Things fall apart.* Greenwich, Connecticut: Fawcett Publications.

Aluko, R. and sherblom, D. (1997). The African immigrant folk life study project at the 1997 Festival, Washington, D. C.: Smithsonian Institute.

Amadi, E. (1973). *Isiburu.* London: Heinemann.

Archer, B. (1980). The arts in education. Arts in Cultural Diversity. Proceedings of INSEA 23rd world congress. Australia: Holt, Rinehart & Winston.

Arts & Life of Africa Online. www.ulowa.edu/~Africa/toc/countries/igbo.html/

Arinze, F. A. (1970). Sacrifice in Ibo religion. Ibadan, Nigeria: Ibadan University Press.

Auchard, J. (1986). Silence in Henry James: The heritage of symbolism and decadence. Pennsylvania: University Press.

Balandier, G. & Maquet, J. (1974). The dictionary of Black African civilization. New York: Leon Amiel.

Banham, M. & Wake, C. (1976). African theater today. London: Pittman.

Banks, J. A. (1997). Teaching strategies for ethnic studies (6th edition). Boston: Allyn and Bacon.

Best, D. (1986). Culture-consciousness: Understanding the arts of other cultures. Journal of Art and Design Education, 5 (1, 2), 33-34.

Bodrogi, T. (1968). Art in Africa. Hungary: Corvina.

Borg, W. & Gall, M. (1983). Educational research: An introduction. (4th ed.). New York: Longman.

Boughton, D. (1986). How do we prepare art teachers for a multicutural society? Journal of Multi-cultural and Cross-cultural Research in Art Education, 4 (1), 94-99.

Borten, H. (1965). Halloween. New York: Thomas Crowell.

Brandon, G. (1997). Yoruba. In Levinson, D. and Ember, M. (Eds.) American immigrant cultures: Builders of a nation (Vol. 2). New York: MacMillan Reference U.S.A.

Bravmann, R. (1974). Islam and tribal art in West Africa. London: Cambridge   University Press.

Broderick, C. (1992). Art communicates individual and society's cultures. Trends, 6(10), 6.

Brook, D. (1980). The unity of art in a diversity of cultures. Arts in cultural diversity.   Proceedings of the INSEA 23rd world congress. Australia: Holt, Rinehart &   Winston.

Burland, C. (1973). Eskimo art. London: Hamlyn.

Calvert, A. E. (1988). Native art history and DBAE: An analysis of key concepts. Journal of Multi-cultural and Cross-cultural Research in Art Education, 6 (1), 112-122.

Carspecken, P. F. & Apple, M. (1992). Critical qualitative research: Theory, methodology and practice. In M. P. LeCompte (Ed.), The handbook of qualitative research in education. San Diego, CA: Academic Press.

Christensen, E. (1985). Primitive art. New York: The Viking Press.

Clark, G. (1990). Art in the schizophrenic fast lane: A response. Art Education, 43 (6), 9-11.

Cole, H. M. & Aniakor, C. C. (1984). Igbo Arts, Community and Cosmos. Los Angeles: University of California Press.

Cook, N. M. & Belanus, B. J. (1997). A taste of home: African immigrant food ways. Washington, D. C.: Smithsonian Institute.

Cordwell, J. M. & Schwarz, R. A. (1979). The fabrics of culture: The anthropology of clothing and adornment. New York: Mouton.

Courtney, R. (1980). The crux of the cultural curriculum: The arts as anthropocentrism. In J. Condous, J. Howlette, and J. Skull, (Eds.), Arts in cultural diversity. Proceedings of the INSEA 23rd World Congress. New York: Holt, Rinehart and Winston.

Dauenhauer, P. B. (1980). Silence: The phenomenon and its ontological significance. Indiana: Indiana University Press.

Davidson, B. (1971). African Kingdoms. Virginia: Time-Life Books.

d'Azevedo, W. L. (1973). The Traditional Artist in African Societies. Bloomington: Indiana University Press.

de Rachewiltz, B. (1966). Introduction to African Art. New York: The New American Library Inc.

Dewey, J. (1980). Art as Experience. New York: G. P. Putnam's.

Dietz, B. W. & Olatunji, M. B. (1965). Musical Instruments of Africa. New York: The John Day Company.

DiBlasio, M. & Park, Y. (1983). Cultural identity and pride through art education: Viewpoint of a Korean-American immigrant community. Journal of Multi-cultural and Cross-cultural Research in Art Education, 1 (1), 33-42.

Duerden, D. (1975). The Invisible Present -- African Art & Literature. New York: Harper & Row.

Fagg, W. (1965). Tribes and Forms in African Art. New York: Tudor.

Fagg, W. & Plass, M. (1964). African Sculpture. London: Studio Vista.

Farris, C. C. (1985). African Rhythms. Arts & Activities, 97 (3), 34-36.

Fehr, D. E. (1994). From theory to practice: Applying the historical context model of art criticism. Art Education, 47 (3). Reston VA: National Art Education Association.

Fehr, D. (1993a). Mona Lisa's Millstone: The modern gods of criticism. Art Education, 46 (1), 68-70. Reston VA: National Art Education Association.

Fehr, D. E. (1993b). Dogs playing cards: Powerbrokers of prejudice in education, art, and culture. New York: Peter Lang.

201

Feldman, E. (1976). Art and the image of the self. Art Education, 29 (5), 10-12.

Fleming, P. S. (1988). Pluralism and DBAE: Towards a model for global multi-cultural art education. Journal of Multi-Cultural and Cross-cultural Research in Art Education, 6 (1), 64-67.

Friedman, M. M. (1998). Family Nursing: Research, theory, and practice. (4th Edition). Stanford, Connecticut: Appleton & Lange.

Gates, F. (1989). North American Indian mask. Colorado: The University Press.

Gay, G. (1986). Multicultural Teacher Education. In J. Banks and J. Lynch. (Eds.). Multicultural education in Western societies. London: Holt, Rinehart & Winston.

Goldwater, R. (1979). Symbolism. New York: Harper & Row Publishers.

Graham-White, A. (1974). The Drama of Black Africa. London: Samuel French.

Grigsby, E. (1989). Emphasizing multicultural aspects in art education [Summary]. Proceedings of a national invitational conference (p. 105). Los Angeles, California: The Getty Center for Education in the Arts.

Grigsby, E. (1986). Using the arts to create bonds between people: The Phoenix experience. Journal of Multi-cultural and Cross-cultural Research in Art Education, 4 (1), 17-29.

Gutek, G. L. (1986). Education in the United States: An historical perspective. New Jersey: Prentice-Hall, Inc.

Hamblen, K. A. (1986). A universal-relative approach to the study of cross-cultural art. Journal of Multi-cultural and Cross-cultural Research in Art Education, 4 (1), 69-77.

Harris, M. (1987). Cultural Anthropology. (2nd edition). New York: Harper & Row.

Harrison, E. R. (1991). A five-year teacher preparation program in art education. Visual Arts Research, 17 (2), 61-65.

Hazard, W. R. & Stent, M. D. (1973). Cultural pluralism and schooling: Some preliminary observations. In M. D. Stent, W. R. Hazard and H. N. Rivlin (Eds.), Cultural pluralism in education: A mandate for change. New York: Appleton-Century-Crofts.

Herold, E. (1967). The Art of Africa---Tribal masks. London: Paul Hamlyn Ltd.

Holmes, E. (1989) Education and Cultural Diversity. New York: Longman.

Huet, M. (1978). The Dance, Art & Ritual of Africa. New York: Pantheon Books.

Hunt, K. & Carlson, B. W. (1961). Masks and Mask Makers. New York: Abingdon Press.

Idowu, E. B. (1975). African Traditional Religion. New York: Orbis Books.

Jefferson, L. E. (1973). The decorative arts of Africa. New York: The Viking press.

Kane. L. (1984). The language of silence. New Jersey: Associated University Press, Inc.

Katter, E. (1991). Meeting the challenge of cultural diversity. Visual Arts Research, 17 (2), 28-32.

King, N. Q. (1970). Religions in Africa. New York: Harper & Row.

Kirby, E. T. (1974). Indigenous African Theater. The Drama Review, 18 (4), 22-34.

Laude, J. (1971). The Arts of Black Africa. Los Angeles: University of California Press.

Laude, J. (1978). Introduction. In M. Huet. The dance, art & ritual of Africa. New York: Pantheon Books.

Lazarus, E. (1989). Equality and Excellence Education in Arts. Design for Arts in Education, 90 (6), 30.

Leuzinger, E. (1960). The Art of Africa. London: Mcgraw-Hill.

Lommel, A. (1970). Masks: Their Meaning and Function. New York: McGraw Hill.

Lovano-Kerr, J. (1985). Cultural Diversity and Art Education: A global perspective. Journal of Multi-cultural and Cross-cultural Research in Art Education, 3 (1), 25.

Mackintosh, A. (1978). Symbolism & Art Nouveau. New York: Barons.

Manning, M. & Baruth, L. G. (1991). Appreciating Cultural Diversity in the Classroom. Kappa Delta Pi Record, 27 (4), 104.

Mbabuike, M. C. (1991). Africa: Art, Culture and Interpretation. Studies in Third World Societies, 46 (1), 65-81.

Mbabuike, M. C. (1991). Ethnicity and Ethnocentrism in the N.Y. Metropolitan area: The case of the Ibos. Studies in Third World Societies, 46 (1), 83-91.

Mbiti, S. (1970). African Religion and Philosophies. New York: Doubleday.

Mbiti, J. S. (1970). Concepts of God in Africa. New York: Praeger.

McGuire, P. (1985). Speechless Dialect: Shakespeare's Open Silences. Los Angeles: University of California Press.

Messenger, J. C. (1973). The role of the carver in Anang society. In W. L. d'Azevedo (Ed.). The Traditional Artists in African Societies. Indiana: Indiana University Press.

Mills, G. (1973). Art and the Anthropological Lens. In W. L. d'Azevedo (Ed.), The Traditional Artist in African Societies. Bloomington: Indiana University Press.

Mitchell, H. H. (1975). Black belief. New York: Harper & Row.

Mittler, G. A. (1986). Art in focus. Peoria, Illinois: Bennett & McKnight.

Nadaner, D. (1985). The Art Teacher as cultural mediator. Journal of Multi-cultural and Cross-cultural Research in Art Education, 3 (1), 51-55.

Napier, D. A. (1986). Masks, Transformations and Paradox. Berkeley, CA: University of California Press.

N'Diaye, D. B. (1997). African Immigrant Culture in Metroploitan Washington, D. C.: Building and Bridging Communities. Washington, D. C.: Smithsonian Institute.

Ogunba, O. (1978). Traditional African festival drama. In O. Ogunba & A. Irele (Eds.), Theater in Africa. Nigeria: Ibadan University Press. pp.-25.
Olumba, A. (1995). "African immigrant folklife study. Fieldwork report."

Ottenberg, S. (1975). Masked rituals of Afikpo: The context of an African art. Seattle: University of Washington Press.

Ottenberg, S. (1960). Cultures and societies of Africa. New York: Random House.

Parrinder, E. G. (1990). African traditional religion. Westport, CT: Greenwood Press.

Picton, J. & Mack, J. (1979). African textiles--looms, weaving & design. London: British Museum Publications.

Ravitch, D. (1992). A culture in common. Educational Leadership, 49 (4), 8.

Richmond, S. (1992). Historicism, teaching, and the understanding of works of art. Visual Arts Research, 18 (1), 32-40.

Rodriguez, F. (1983). Education in a Multicultural Society. Washington, DC: University   Press of America.

Rodrigues, G. (1974). Ritual dolls and figurines of Black Africa. African ritual dolls.   Philadelphia: University Museum.

Ryan, T. (1988). Holderlin's silence. New York: Peter Long.

Schmalenbach, W. (1988). African Art. Munich: Prestel-Verlag.
Schools remove arts. NAEA News, 33 (4), 1-2.

Segy, L. (1976). Masks of Black Africa. New York: Dover Publications.

Selassie, B. (1996). Washington's new African immigrants. In Carey, Frances (Ed.) Urban Odyssey: Migration to Washington, D. C. Washington, D. C.: Smithsonian Institute Press.

Sieber, R. (1980). African furniture and household objects. Bloomington: Indiana University.

Sieber, R. (1974). Interaction: The art styles of the Benue River Valley and East Nigeria. Purdue: Creative Arts Department, Purdue University.

Sieber, R. (1973). Approaches to non-Western art. In W. L. d'Azevedo (Ed.). The traditional artist in African societies. Bloomington: Indiana University Press.

Smith, R. A. (1980). Celebrating the arts in their cultural diversity: Some wrong and right ways to do it. Arts in cultural diversity. Proceedings of the INSEA 23rd world   congress. Australia: Holt, Rinehart & Winston.

Soyinka, W. (1976). Myth, literature and the African world. London: Cambridge.

Speer, T. L. (1995). A cracked door: U. S. policy welcomes only Africa's brightest and richest. Emerge. 6 (9), 36.

Speer, T. (1994). The newest African Americans aren't Black. American Demographics. 16 (1), 9-10.

Spencer, H. (1966). What knowledge is most worth? In M. A. Kazamias (Ed.), Herbert Spencer on education (pp. 121-159). New York: Teachers College Press.

Splinder G. & Splinder L. (1965). Foreword. In V. C. Uchendu. The Igbo of Southeast Nigeria. New York: Holt, Rinehart & Winston.

Spradley, J. P. (1979). The ethnographic interview. New York: Holt, Rinehart and   Winston.

Srozenski, B. (1991). Nigerian culture and religion. Art and culture in Nigeria and the Dispora, 46 (1), 143-155.

Takaki, R. (1993). A different mirror: A history of multicultural America. Boston: Little, Brown & Company.

Tannen, D. & Saville-Troike, M. (1985). Perspectives on silence. New Jersey: Ablex.

Tanner, D. & Tanner, L. N. (1980). Curriculum development (2nd ed.). New York: Macmillan.

Tanner, D. & Tanner, L. (1990). History of the school curriculum. New York: Macmillan.

The Junior League of Houston (1995). West Africa: Houston International Festival 1996 Curriculum Guide.

Thompson, R. F. (1974). African Art in Motion. Los Angeles, California: University of California Press.

Tomhave, R. D. (1992). Value bases underlying conceptions of multicultural education: An analysis of selected literature in art education. Studies in Art Education, 34 (1), 48-60.

Uchendu, V. C. (1965). The Igbo of Southeast Nigeria. New York: Holt, Rinehart & Winston.

Umez, B. (2001). The Only Savior for Africa: Liberate African Mind. The Houston Punch. February 2001.

Umezinwa, W. A. (1980). The idiom of plastic figures in Achebe's novels. Nsukka Studies in African Literature, 3 (3), 13-21.

Ungar, S. J. (1995). Fresh Blood: The New American Immigrants. New York: Simon & Schuster.

Vevers, T. (1974). Interaction: The art styles of the Benue river valley and East Nigeria. Purdue: Purdue University.

Willet, F. (1985). African art: An introduction. New York: Thames &Hudson.

Willet, F. (1971). The traditional art of African nations. New York: University Publishers.

Woodhead, H. (1992). The spirit world. Alexandra: Time-Life Books.

Wynn, R. (1995). Immigration Woes. The Tennessee Tribune 5 (7), 11-12.

INDEX

209

210

Igbo art, 137, 218, 219, 220, 242, 244, 245, 249, 253, 274, 287, 296, 299, 300, 301, 306, 307, 330, 334, 340, 373, 400, 409, 412

Igbo artists, 218, 307

Igbo calendar, 211

Igbo mask, 207, 211, 234, 242, 243, 256, 257, 258, 259, 262, 268, 306, 338

Igrube, 55, 56

Ikenga, 41, 274, 275, 282, 392

Ikoro, 43, 44

Incantation, 260, 322, 367

Inclusion relationship, 280

Invisible, 41, 217, 255, 259, 263, 277, 278, 281, 299, 303, 312, 354, 363, 364, 413

Invitation, 194, 255, 415

Irish, 83

Japanese, 83

Jews, 83

Jobs, 14, 84, 86, 87, 89, 90, 157

Kite, 3, 298, 310, 356, 400

Koboko, 44, 45, 46, 48, 49, 50, 51

Kolanut, 16, 17, 41, 126, 127, 128, 129, 151,   171, 216, 256, 261, 322, 324, 325, 326, 327, 357, 358, 359, 360, 361, 362, 384, 400

Machete, 6, 69, 158, 287

Male, 119, 158, 162, 197, 211, 226, 257, 388, 389, 391,

Male drum, 369

Malevolent, 203, 254, 316, 388, 396, 397

Mainstream, 93, 103, 105, 106, 197

Manhood, 16, 56, 172

Man-regarding, 204, 208, 388, 398, 399

Marriage, 16, 17, 148, 154, 163, 176, 186, 187, 188, 189, 344, 391

Mask, 137 – 407

Mask carving, 207, 208, 241, 242, 247, 256, 287, 338, 394, 397

Mask dancer, 260, 261, 340

Masquerade, 5, 6, 108, 118, 133, 137, 139, 140, 141, 172, 212, 229, 230, 231, 238, 239, 241, 248, 249, 250, 251, 260, 261, 263, 302, 315, 317, 319, 329, 331, 334, 335, 336, 337, 339, 341, 342, 343, 369, 373, 374, 376, 378, 379, 386, 387, 394, 407

Masquerade society, 248, 249, 260

Migrating, 89

Migration, 85, 421

Mother Earth, 1, 3, 17, 28, 126, 141, 212, 287, 311, 312, 321, 355, 361, 370, 377, 385, 390, 398

New Yam, 1, 3, 7, 122, 132, 133, 136, 231, 243, 283, 287, 321, 322, 323, 370, 410

New Yam Festival, 1, 3, 7, 122, 231, 243, 321, 370, 401

Nigeria, 8, 75, 85, 94, 117, 122, 156, 157, 170, 171, 184, 204, 205, 209, 213, 215, 222, 325, 326, 360, 410, 419, 421, 422, 423, 424

Oduduwa, 110, 111, 213

Oji, 256 - 258

Okonko, 248, 249, 327, 329, 331, 333, 334, 364, 368, 369, 370, 372, 373

Old age, 148, 150, 264, 265, 336, 388, 398, 403

Onny, 8, 63, 65, 73, 401, 402, 403, 404, 405

Oranmiyan, 111

Palm-fronds, 6, 337

Palm oil, 41, 55, 168, 174, 210

Palm-wine, 5, 16, 17, 18, 41, 42, 120, 151, 256, 261, 322

Pearls of Nile Valley, 109

Pogroms, 83, 84, 94

Political greed, 94

Political instability, 86, 222

Poverty, 73, 83, 84, 94, 195

Professor, 87, 92, 158, 176, 227

Prophet, 236, 284, 302, 385

Racism, 89

Religion, 41, 146, 190, 191, 202, 203, 209, 213, 235, 246, 272, 276, 277, 283, 287, 318, 352, 386, 390, 410, 416, 417, 418, 420, 422

Respect, 10, 19, 102, 112, 127, 132, 143, 147, 148, 149, 150, 151, 153, 159, 160, 182, 188, 191, 216, 229, 236, 257, 265, 295, 370, 383, 389, 403, 404

Ritual, 2, 41, 58, 108, 114, 116, 117, 124, 125, 128, 129, 130, 131, 135, 138, 139, 143, 150, 151, 172, 187, 191, 192, 207, 208, 209, 211, 216, 217, 220, 221, 222, 225, 226, 231, 235, 236, 241, 244, 248, 252, 253, 254, 255, 260, 261, 267, 268, 270, 275, 277, 284, 285, 291, 293, 296, 299, 300, 301, 302, 304, 306, 307, 309, 311, 312, 313, 314, 315, 317, 318, 319, 320, 321, 323, 327, 328, 329, 332, 333, 335, 341, 242, 343, 344, 350, 352, 354, 357, 358, 363, 364, 366, 367, 368, 371, 373, 377, 378, 380, 381, 383, 384, 385, 388, 389,

SYMPOSIUM SERIES